Reducing criminality among young people: a sample of relevant programmes in the United Kingdom

by
David Utting

A Research and Statistics Directorate Report

Home Office
Research and
Statistics
Directorate

London: Home Office

1858937442

Home Office Research Studies

The Home Office Research Studies are reports on research undertaken by or on behalf of the Home Office. They cover the range of subjects for which the Home Secretary has responsibility. Titles in the series are listed at the back of this report (copies are available from the address on the back cover). Other publications produced by the Research and Statistics Directorate include Research Findings, the Research Bulletin, Statistical Bulletins and Statistical Papers.

The Research and Statistics Directorate

The Directorate consists of three Units which deal with research and statistics on Crime and Criminal Justice, Offenders and Corrections, Immigration and General Matters; the Programme Development Unit; the Economics Unit; and the Operational Research Unit.

 The Research and Statistics Directorate is an integral part of the Home Office, serving the Ministers and the department itself, its services, Parliament and the public through research, development and statistics. Information and knowledge from these sources informs policy development and the management of programmes; their dissemination improves wider public understanding of matters of Home Office concern.

First published 1996

Application for reproduction should be made to the Information and Publications Group, Room 1308, Home Office, Apollo House, 36 Wellesley Road, Croydon CR9 3RR.

©Crown copyright 1996 ISBN 1 85893 744 2
ISSN 0072 6435

Foreword

This study was commissioned by the Home Office Research and Statistics Directorate with three main objectives:

- to report on current initiatives that are relevant to reducing criminality in the areas of parent education and family support, schools and sport and leisure activities

- to provide descriptions of the design, cost and effectiveness of promising projects in each of the three areas

- to identify the main features of good practice.

Thanks are due to all the organisations whose work is described in the report and to the many individuals and agencies (listed in Chapter one) who provided the author with useful information and advice.

CHRIS LEWIS
Head of Offenders and Corrections Unit

Contents

1 Introduction

What distinguishes the lives of children and young people who become criminals from those who manage to stay out of trouble and respect the law? Researchers in Britain, the United States and other 'western' nations have devoted considerable time and energy during the past 50 years to trying to expose 'the roots of delinquency'.[1] Comparisons between the backgrounds, circumstances, behaviour and attitudes of individuals have identified thousands of different risk factors that distinguish those who commit crime from non-offenders–and which do so in ways that are statistically more than a matter of chance (Farrington, 1996). But this does not mean they necessarily represent the underlying causes of delinquency.

Studies that analyse the most significant factors identifying children and young people at increased risk of criminality (somewhat misleadingly known in statistics as 'predictors') have helped to narrow the field (Loeber and Dishion, 1983; Loeber, Stouthamer and Loeber, 1986). Researchers do not always agree on their relative strengths but in summary they include:

Personal risk factors	Hyperactivity/high impulsivity Low intelligence
Family risk factors	Poor parental supervision Harsh or erratic discipline Parental conflict Separation from a biological parent Parent with a criminal record
Socio-economic and community risk factors	Low income Poor housing Living in public housing in inner cities Socially disorganised community
Educational risk factors	Low attainment Aggressive/troublesome behaviour in school.

---

1. This was the title adopted for a study of the social backgrounds of young people who became offenders in the longitudinal National Survey of Health and Development of children born in Britain in 1946 (see Wadswoth, M. 1979).

A range of protective factors has, likewise, been observed that appear to buffer children and young people, including those in socially disadvantaged neighbourhoods, from developing anti-social behaviour and acquiring a criminal record. (Rutter and Giller, 1983; Kolvin et al., 1990). In many cases they are the polar opposites of risk factors, and include high intelligence, consistent parental discipline and supervision and a good level of achievement in school. When assembling the overall picture it becomes increasingly apparent that the extent that children are able to form positive, pro-social attachments at different stages of their development–first with their parent(s) and families, thereafter with their schools and communities–is crucial (Sampson and Laub, 1993; Smith, 1995; Howell et al., 1995).

Most of the main risk factors tend to coincide and be inter-related. This creates difficulties in establishing their independent significance as influences on offending and anti-social behaviour. For example, it is evident that young people who mix with criminal friends are more likely to be criminal themselves, but it is not clear whether membership of a delinquent peer group is a cause or a symptom (or both) of their offending. However, young people living in run-down and socially disorganised neighbourhoods tend, disproportionately, to come from families with poor parental supervision and erratic parental discipline and also to display high impulsivity and low intelligence (Farrington, 1996). Nor is it difficult to see how low income and disadvantaged living conditions might influence parenting and how parents under stress might, in turn, influence the development of high impulsivity and aggression in their children.

Although it is not possible to single out any one factor as 'the cause of criminality', it is apparent that as adverse circumstances cluster together in a child's background, so the odds against later criminal involvement grow shorter (West, 1982). There is also evidence that where factors such as poor supervision, harsh discipline and low income are experienced by children at their most extreme, there is an increased risk that they will grow into recidivist offenders, responsible for a disproportionate volume of crime (Osborn and West, 1978). Children who start their criminal careers early – before the age of 14–are especially likely to persist as offenders, committing multiple offences (Patterson, 1994a and 1994b).

Combinations of factors can be used to recognise children and young people whose chances of later criminal involvement are disproportionately high. Such 'predictors' must be treated with caution, however, since they may apply to so narrow a group that they fail to identify the vast majority of subsequent offenders ('false negatives'). Likewise, those that point to a broader band of population are in danger of labelling a substantial proportion of children as 'potential offenders' who will not, in reality, become criminally involved at all ('false positives') (Utting et al., 1983). For example, anti-social behaviour among children is one of the strongest 'predictors' of anti-social behaviour in adults, but it is also true that only a minority of anti-social children grow up that way (Robins, 1978).

Recent reviews of the research literature have argued that although proper attention must be paid to the pitfalls involved in targeting initiatives, considerable scope exists for interventions whose aim is to prevent crime by reducing criminality. As the House of Commons Home Affairs Committee reported in 1993:

> "..investment in identifying and eliminating the causes of crime is clearly preferable to paying for the damage once it has been done,"

The authors of the Home Office study of *Young People and Crime* concluded that efforts to prevent young people from becoming involved in crime should focus on:

- strengthening families–for example, by parent training, family centres and support groups, and specific measures for lone parents and step-families,

- strengthening schools–for example, by strategies to prevent truanting and developing practical measures to improve family–school relationships

- protecting young people (particularly young men) from the influence of delinquents in their peer group and from high risk activities such as alcohol and drug abuse

- harnessing the sources of social control within the criminal justice system to the more informal sources of control found among families, schools and neighbours

- preparing young people for fully independent and responsible adulthood.(Graham and Bowling, 1995).

A 1995 report by Crime Concern, the national crime prevention charity, suggested that the prevention of criminality has received relatively little attention in the United Kingdom compared with 'situational' measures designed to make crime more difficult to commit (Crime Concern 1995).

It would, nevertheless, be wrong to suppose that there are no existing examples of criminality prevention (also known as 'social crime prevention') programmes in Britain.

- The local boards of Safer Cities and other community safety initiatives have begun to include relevant projects such as parenting education, anti-bullying schemes and youth activity programmes as part of their strategies. Other innovative projects have been sponsored in recent years by the Home Office Programme Development Unit.

- The Children Act 1989 not only requires local authorities to support children in families under stress, but also gives them a specific duty to take measures that discourage juvenile involvement in crime.

- There is a wide range of work by statutory and voluntary organisations that is relevant to the prevention of anti-social behaviour, even though criminality reduction is not its main focus. For example, a nursery school providing disadvantaged children with a high standard of pre-school education is unlikely to specify crime prevention among its objectives, even though research identifies the link.

- The boundaries for initiatives designed to prevent reoffending by known juvenile offenders and those aimed at young people on the fringes of a criminal career are frequently blurred. Youth projects such as those using outdoor adventure activities to teach pro-social behaviour and personal skills are often made available to young people 'at risk' as well as to known offenders.

This report

The central purpose of this report is to describe a selection of promising work in the United Kingdom that is relevant to reducing criminality among young people. This is provided under three specific headings:

- Families

- Schools

- Sport and leisure.

Each chapter is prefaced by a short summary of the research that allows these different types of work to be considered collectively as criminality reduction programmes. Those wanting a more detailed account of the available evidence should refer to the cited publications.

The projects described in the three central chapters of this report are located in the United Kingdom. They have not (with notable exceptions) been rigorously evaluated, but all of them have demonstrated a degree of promise that justifies their inclusion. Some are adaptations of programmes that originate and have been evaluated in

America. Where this is the case, information has been provided on the parent projects as well. In addition to descriptive information, an indication is given of the cost of each project and sources of funding. However, there are differences in the ways that programmes are costed and no reliable comparisons of cost effectiveness have been possible.

The report does not attempt to provide a comprehensive survey of relevant projects. The aim has been to illustrate the range of existing work, not its depth. In selecting 'promising' programmes for inclusion, the author has supplemented his own knowledge and a review of relevant literature with advice from organisations and individual specialists. These include:

- Barnardos

- The Children's Society

- Crime Concern

- The Divert Trust

- Institute of Leisure and Amenity Management

- NACRO

- National Youth Council

- NCH–Action for Children

- Sports Council

- Cambridgeshire County Council (Community Education)

- Hampshire Probation/Youth Justice Service

- Inner London Probation Service

- Kent County Council (Youth Justice)

- South Glamorgan County Council (Youth Justice)

- Gerard Bates (South Glamorgan Probation Service)

- Jon Barrett (Basecamp)

- Fred Coalter (Centre for Leisure Research, Herriott-Watt University)

- Professor David Farrington (Institute of Criminology, Cambridge)

- John Huskins (Former HMI, Schools)

- Valerie Jones (London Borough of Redbridge)

- Michael Little (Dartington Hall)

- Professor Peter Mortimore (Institute of Education, London University)

- Gillian Pugh (National Children's Bureau)

- David Robins (Author: 'Sport as Crime Prevention')

- Andrew Walls (DfEE, Attendance & Discipline Division).

To assist in identifying elements of good practice, a number of programmes have been singled out for longer description and additional comment by the author.

2 Families

Introduction

From the time of conception there are aspects of a baby's family background that will influence its future well-being. This chapter is concerned with practical ways in which the right intervention at the right time in a child's life can reduce the risks of later criminal involvement. The sample of parenting and family support programmes it describes covers a developmental span from infancy to adolescence.

Interventions whose aim is to strengthen families and improve the quality of child-rearing are likely to yield multiple preventive benefits. This is an important source of strength, but it does mean that reducing the risks of criminality will not necessarily be acknowledged as an objective (Utting et al., 1993). Smoking, drinking alcohol and illegal drug abuse during pregnancy have, for example, been associated with low birth weight and perinatal complications that are, in turn, linked to later conduct problems and delinquency (Farrington, 1996). But there are more pressing health reasons for persuading expectant mothers to give up smoking and to make full use of ante-natal care services than an added risk of criminality more than ten years hence.

The programmes in this chapter have been selected because they address the most significant family risk factors identified by research. These are:

- poor parental supervision

- parental neglect

- harsh or erratic discipline

- parental conflict

- long-term separation from a biological parent

- having a parent with a criminal record.

Besides addressing family factors, some programmes are also concerned with the various personal, educational, socio-economic and community risk factors associated with criminality.

The programmes range from those that are generally available, to others that are highly specialised and intended for parents and children under severe stress.

They are categorised as follows (see Utting et al., 1993):

- Universal services–offered to any parent or family who might find them helpful:

    Exploring Parenthood (Check it Out! Moyenda Project)
    Kids' Clubs Network
    Parent Network
    Parents As Teachers

- Neighbourhood services–available to families under stress and/or living within a targeted area of disadvantage:

    Exploring Parenthood (Parents Against Crime)
    Home-Start
    West Leeds Family Service Unit
    Parent Network (Parent-Link Family Centre, Exeter)
    Pen Green Centre (Corby)

- Family Preservation–'intensive care' interventions aimed at families where relationships are under severe stress, including those where children may otherwise be taken into care.[1] Family preservation services tend to be 'eleventh hour' interventions offered close to the point of breakdown. Nevertheless, there is an assumption that the cost will be lower than allowing the next crisis point to be reached:

    Family Nurturing Network
    Maudsley Hospital Child and Adolescent Psychiatry Department;
    Mellow Parenting
    NEWPIN
    Radford Shared Care (Nottingham).

The *Young Offender Community Support Scheme* in Hampshire and the *Community Placement* and *Remand Fostering Schemes* in South Glamorgan might also be included under this heading, although their task is

---

1. A number of family preservation services exist with the object of strengthening family functioning so that the threat of care proceedings for children 'at risk' can be removed. The relationship between young people's care experiences and criminality is not straightforward (Hardiker, P.; Exton, K. & Barker, M. 1991). Yet the knowledge that an altogether disproportionate number of inmates in Young Offender Institutions (Home Office Research and Statistics Department, 1991) have a care history argues the preventive sense, as well as the cost-effectiveness, of keeping children out of care where possible.

to place young people with foster families. This is done in the expectation that experiencing life in a stable home can prevent or reduce behavioural problems and criminal activity.

Universal Services

Exploring parenthood

Brief description: the organisation provides advice and counselling to parents through a national telephone helpline and runs group programmes for families under stress. It also offers training for agencies wanting to provide parental skills education, including those involved in crime prevention and community safety programmes. Projects in the recent past have included a small, pilot *Parents Against Crime* programme for parents of children in trouble with the law, a workplace information service for parents and an information and support programme for black and Asian families.

Location: the *Parents Against Crime* project was based in West London. The workplace information service *(Check it Out)* was provided for employees of the IKEA chain of furniture stores. The *Moyenda Project* works with black and Asian families in various localities in London, Luton and the South East.

Referrals: families of young people aged 10 and over who participated in the *Parents Against Crime* programme were referred by the police in North Kensington or by social services. The *Check it Out* service was available to all IKEA employees. Participants in short courses and workshops run by *the Moyenda Project* are contacted through community groups, churches and media publicity.

Programmes: families took part in *Parents Against Crime* voluntarily. The programme included a weekly support group meeting for six sessions where parents discussed listening skills, negotiating boundaries for children, assertiveness, discipline, adolescence and advice on dealing with the police, social services and other agencies. The young people 'known to the police' were encouraged to take part in a youth group designed to confront their offending behaviour and to introduce them to constructive leisure activities. *Check it Out* was a wide-ranging personal advice service provided by advisers making weekly visits to IKEA stores. Nearly half the problems on which staff sought help related to personal relationships or parenting. *The Moyenda Project* has organised a number of small groups and workshops bringing together Asian and black parents, mostly mothers. These include discussion of general parenting concerns and issues of parenting style within their particular communities. A pilot programme for black fathers has recently been introduced, including sessions on role models, the value of fathering, relationships with partners and coping with poor prospects and racism. Small-scale sample surveys have been carried out to assess the support needs of black parents. The project has identified white parents of black children as a group who come under exceptional stress.

Outcomes: *Parents Against Crime* existed for 12 months from January 1993. Two parent support groups were run during the year with the participation of a maximum of eight parents and seven young people, and six parents and five young people, respectively. Attendance at individual sessions was variable. Parents and project staff felt the programme had led to greater understanding of child development and increased confidence in supervising their children–although a more positive impact was noted on relations between parents and their younger children than with their delinquent sons. Project staff told researchers that the adolescents attending were more 'damaged' or 'hardened' than anticipated. It was concluded that a six week programme was too brief to work effectively with parents and that therapeutic work with juvenile offenders required highly experienced youth workers (Henricson,1995; De Souza, 1994).

Check it Out was used by 22 per cent of IKEA's 400 staff in London–double the take up achieved by companies that have previously offered in-house advice services to their employees. There was a high take up by fathers as well as mothers and the service was valued as a 'one-stop shop' for gaining access to more specialist help if necessary (Burnell, 1995). The project led Exploring Parenthood to launch a 'Work and Family' service that is nationally available to employers.

Organisers of The *Moyenda Project*, which began in 1991, say it has allowed them to develop a culturally sensitive model for working with black parents. Although attendance at courses has been variable, there has been a high level of demand from community groups around the country. An evaluation report recommended that black families should have greater access to culturally appropriate information on parenting and parent support groups (Exploring Parenthood,1995).

Funding and costs: *Parents Against Crime* was funded for one year by the Home Office and other charitable sources. Including research and administration, it cost £21,400. *Check it Out* received a grant of £120,000 from the Joseph Rowntree Foundation.

The Moyenda Project was funded by a grant of £14,000 a year for three years from the Department of Health and £5,000 a year each from the Lord Ashdown Foundation and the Carnegie Trust.

Kids' Clubs Network

Brief description: the organisation promotes childcare for school age children and provides a national training and support agency for the rapidly increasing number of out-of-school clubs around the country. Its immediate concern is to provide children with stimulating play opportunities and to support parents–especially those who work. But it is also explicit in arguing that after-school clubs can contribute to crime prevention by enabling children to play safely and reducing the incidence of petty crime and vandalism.

Location: Kids' Clubs Network is based in London with 12 local offices in England and Wales. More than a third of clubs are based in schools, but the remainder use family centres, community centres, church halls or their own premises. A quarter provide childcare before, as well as after, school and many during the holidays. Most are voluntary organisations run by management boards of parents and community leaders, but one in five operate as small or community businesses. Some are run directly by local authorities.

Referrals: club membership is usually open to children aged 5 to 12. Some reserve spaces for children 'in need' including those at risk of physical or sexual abuse.

Programmes: clubs are normally staffed by qualified play workers and volunteer parents. Play workers collect children from school and escort them to the club where they are registered, given tea and encouraged to take part in a wide range of activities including arts and crafts, games, sport, drama, music and storytelling. Clubs run all-day programmes during the school holidays, including special events and outings.

Outcomes: the number of out - of - school clubs and holiday playschemes has quadrupled from just over 600 to more than 3,000 in the past three years, encouraged by the launch in 1993 of the Department of Employment's *Out of School Initiative.* Approximately 70,000 places are provided for up to 120,000 children (Kids' Clubs Network, 1995). An evaluation by Sussex University researchers of development work on 13 pilot initiatives funded by the Department of Health noted a distinction between clubs relying heavily on subsidy and volunteers (concentrated in disadvantage urban areas) and those run on business lines, charging a market rate for places (more often found in middle-class areas). It concluded that many of the projects showed promise, but that voluntary organisations needed more help to ensure their sustainability over time (Warren and Hartless, 1996). An evaluation for the DfEE, focusing on parental employment outcomes, found that 40 per cent of parents using a club for up to a year had improved their employment prospects(Dept. for Education and Employment, 1996).

Funding and costs: Kids' Clubs Network estimate the cost of a model club, with places for 24 children at around £50,000 a year. This is broken down to a cost of £32 a week per place during term time and £64 a week during the holidays. Many clubs offer subsidised places to low income families or with more than one child, so that the average fee to parents is £15 a week after-school and £35 a week in the holidays (Kids' Club Network, 1995). Out - of - school clubs often depend on a number of funders including local authorities, Training and Enterprise Councils (TECs), charitable foundations and private companies. Central government support has included the *Out of School Childcare Initiative* which has provided £45 million through TECs over three years towards start-up costs and first year administration. A further £12.5 million was committed by DfEE for the next three years. The Department of Health provided £5 million for its *Out of School Childcare Project* which funded 13 demonstration schemes between 1992 and 1995. Money for kids' clubs has also been obtained locally through the Safer Cities initiative, Opportunities for Volunteering, the Single Regeneration Budget and the EU Social Fund.

Parent Network

Brief description: Parent Network is a parent education organisation that aims to 'help improve the quality of family life and reduce the likelihood of family breakdown or divorce'. Its basic *Parent-Link* course–sometimes characterised as 'a toolkit for parents'–is considered suitable for parents (and grandparents) caring for children of any age.

Location: the national organisation started in 1986. Although its 200 facilitators work in 30 areas stretching from Aberdeen to Cornwall, its coverage remains patchy. Many groups are run privately, but some local authorities have offered Parent-Link in community centres, schools and as part of their adult education programme. Groups have also been run in Brixton and Holloway prisons and a Parent-Link Family Centre has been established on a large estate in Exeter (see below).

Referrals: parents normally make contact themselves, and organisers commonly rely on local advertising and word of mouth. Individuals may be put in touch with local groups by health visitors, GPs, social workers and other professionals.

Programme: *Parent-Link* is a 13-week course that follows a published curriculum including skills such as listening to children, talking about feelings, solving problems and resolving conflict. Emphasis is placed on setting boundaries and disciplining children in a consistent, but non-violent manner. Parents are encouraged to be assertive, using 'I messages' to make clear statements of what they do and do not like – rather than labelling children in general terms as 'naughty' or 'good'. The stated aim is to be a 'good enough', as opposed to 'perfect', parent. Unlike more directive parent training programmes in the United States, the first part of each session provides an opportunity for parents to talk informally about particular problems they have encountered. The co-ordinators are parents who have undergone a six-month training programme in addition to the Parent-Link course. Their role is intended to be that of an experienced fellow-parent, rather than 'teacher'. Follow-up courses include a 'Living with Teenagers' programme and workshops on 'stress management', 'sibling rivalry', 'being a father' and 'anger management'.

- The *Parent-Link Family Centre* in Exeter serves a large council estate with a high proportion of low income and vulnerable families. The range of activities include a mother and toddler club, a pre-school playgroup, holiday playschemes, craft workshops, a drop-in day for parents, a toy library and baby equipment loan scheme, a child development group, a young mothers' group and confidential counselling for parents under stress. Parents who attend the centre can join a weekly group pursuing the Parent-Link course. The only charges are for the handbooks (£10) and use of the crèche facilities, if required.

Outcomes: an estimated 12,000 parents have attended a Parent-Link course at some time in the past ten years. Questionnaires completed by participants before and after a course funded by the London Borough of Waltham Forest showed that parents reported a better understanding of their children's feelings and emotional needs. They also felt the programme had helped them to communicate better and to manage their children's behaviour more effectively (Baginsky, 1993). An external evaluation of Parent-Link, by Dr Hilton Davies of the Child and Adolescent Unit of Psychiatry and Psychology at Guys Medical Centre, has found that more than 90 per cent of parents who complete the course feel more confident and consider they have learned new skills. Over 70 per cent say they have observed significant improvements in their children's behaviour.(Davis, 1996). Parent Network's own monitoring in the early 1990s suggested that the majority of parents taking its courses were white and middle class (ABC1s). Fathers were heavily outnumbered by mothers. The organisation, however, claims success for a number of courses for parents from Asian and Afro-Caribbean ethnic backgrounds (Utting et al., 1993).

Funding and costs: fees for private Parent-Link courses are charged by the co-ordinators and range between £70 and £100 per person including copies of the curriculum handbooks. Where Parent Network has worked under contract with a local authority, Parent-Link has been offered free or at a reduced charge. The family centre in Exeter uses NHS-owned premises and is jointly funded by the Devon Social Services and Community Education departments and by the Children in Need charity. Running costs for 1995–6 were £36,360.

Parents as Teachers UK

Brief description: Parents as Teachers is a school-based programme that brings parents of children aged 0 to 3 together to learn more about parenting, child development and early learning. The 'parent counsellors' running the programme also make home visits. They are not necessarily teachers, but one important aim of the programme is to foster home–school links.

Location: developed in Missouri in the United States, it has spread to 40 other US states and has a small but increasing presence in Britain. It was introduced to the UK in 1992 by the head teacher of Kings Wood First School in High Wycombe and is now established at six other schools in Buckinghamshire, Hertfordshire, Sandwell and Tower Hamlets. The latter project is part of a parent literacy project incorporated in a *Cities in Schools* (see Chapter 3) prevention programme.

Referrals: the programme is open to any parents of children aged 3 and under who wish to attend. Recruitment methods used by Pam Holtom, the head teacher at Kings Wood, have included a leaflet for parents of new-born babies in the school's catchment area and letters to parents when they enrol their children for school entry.

Programme: meetings are held fortnightly for parents to meet each other and consider a wide range of parenting topics ranging from conflict and behaviour and discipline to potty training, choosing a playgroup, and child health and nutrition. A manual gives the counsellors running these sessions guidance on how to introduce helpful ideas and stimulate discussion. Counsellors also visit families in their own homes, offering advice on a one-to-one basis and suggesting developmentally appropriate play ideas and activities.

Outcomes: Parents as Teachers in Missouri works with more than 60,000 parents a year. Evaluation suggests that although universally available, it has helped a disproportionate number of disadvantaged families including lone parents, fathers lacking educational qualifications and social security claimants. The unexpectedly high proportion of parenting problems found among comparatively well educated, two-parent families has underlined one of the potential benefits of making parent education universally accessible.

After three years, parental knowledge of child development was shown to have increased significantly for participants, while measures of children's language skills and achievement produced an average score above the national norm (this, despite a higher than average level of social disadvantage among parents) (Pfannensteil et al., 1991).

The programme at Kings Wood School in High Wycombe has more than 60 parents involved and the average attendance at meetings is over 20. A Punjabi-speaking volunteers has been running parallel sessions for Asian parents. The head teacher's impression is that a strong relationship is being forged between parents and the school that will benefit children when they begin compulsory education. She believes the programme is especially acceptable to parents because it is non-stigmatising and identifies with giving children an educational head start.

Funding and costs: Parents as Teachers in the UK has, to date, made extensive use of volunteer and existing school staff. The estimated cost of starting a new project with an accredited parent consultant holding a nursery nurse (NNEB) qualification and working part-time is just under £5,000 a year, plus start-up costs of £2,000. With a caseload of 30 families, the unit running cost per family would be £166 a year.

Neighbourhood Services

Home-Start

Brief description: Home-Start uses trained volunteers who are experienced parents to offer friendship, practical advice and support to families with pre-school children. According to the guidance accompanying the Children Act, it is an example of services that *'offer parents under stress significant amounts of time from volunteers who are likely to be seen as friends with no power or tradition of interfering in family life and who may themselves have surmounted similar difficulties'.* (Department of Health, 1991). Since it began over 20 years ago in Leicester, the idea of Home-Start has been exported to Australia, Canada, Hungary, the Irish Republic, Israel, The Netherlands and Norway. It is also active among the families of British forces stationed in Cyprus and Germany.

Location: a network of more than 180 autonomous home visiting schemes around the country is supported by a national consultancy, Home-Start UK.

Referrals: Home-Start works alongside the statutory health and social services helping families whose problems include post-natal stress, parental conflict, domestic violence and suspected child abuse[2] as well as money

---

2.   It is a rule that where volunteers discover suspected abuse they notify Social Services, rather than attempting to deal with it themselves.

problems, children's behavioural problems and more general difficulties coping with the demands of a young family. Referrals come from health visitors, doctors, social workers, teachers and other professionals as well as voluntary organisations such as RELATE, Stepfamily or Gingerbread. Parents themselves may ask for a volunteer to visit them. Visiting is open-ended and the only conditions for beginning are that:

* the family includes at least one child aged under five

* the family wants to be visited.

Programme: Home-Start does not specify crime prevention or reducing the risks of criminality among its objectives. Its aim – stated simply – is "helping to prevent family crisis and breakdown and emphasise the pleasures of family life". Its role is defined as one of increasing the confidence and independence of families with children under five who are experiencing frustrations or difficulties. To this end its volunteers aim to:

* visit families in their own homes where the problems exist

* develop a relationship where there is mutual understanding

* share their practical skills as parents

* build on the existing strengths of parents, respecting their dignity and encouraging them to show confidence in their own abilities

* reassure parents that it is not unusual to encounter problems in bringing up children

* encourage families to widen their network of friends in the community and make effective use of available services.[3]

The approach varies according to the needs of individual families. Volunteers must be prepared to roll up their sleeves to help bring order to a chaotic home, play with children (modelling discipline and other parenting skills in the process) or simply to lend a sympathetic ear to a mother who is lonely and depressed. Common needs are for parents to be given a break to do housework or to devote more time to a particular child. Visits usually take place once or twice a week, but may be more frequent at a time of crisis. The support requested from a volunteer is likely to vary over time. Other typical activities include accompanying families on outings or helping them

---

3.   Adapted from the Standards and Methods of Practice included in -Home Start's model constitution.

to keep appointments. Volunteers also find themselves called upon to 'mother' young, single parents who lack support from their own families. By encouraging parents to discover and build on their own strengths, they aim to ensure that their advice on parenting, family management and other matters is both acceptable and accepted (Shinman, 1994).

In addition to its paid organiser, each Home-Start scheme can usually call on about 30 volunteers. The intention is to recruit experienced parents from a wide range of backgrounds. Parents who have been visited often become volunteers themselves. No prior qualifications are demanded, but all volunteers must complete a ten-week training course that includes:

• basic child development theory

• the ethics of visiting people in their own homes

• understanding and building relationships

• knowledge of other locally available support services.

Volunteers are usually matched with one or two families, but no more than three at any one time.

Outcomes: national monitoring shows that in 1995–6 Home-Start schemes in Britain supported more than 11,400 families of which more than a third were headed by a lone parent. The 27,270 children being visited included 924 whose names appeared on child protection registers. In March 1996, there were more than 4,600 Home-Start volunteers with another 665 attending training courses. Home-Start has been the subject of a number of research studies:

• A survey of 90 user families found that half had been referred to Home-Start by health visitors and most had been visited for between six months to a year. Six out of ten mothers were 'very satisfied' with the service received and half specified beneficial changes in their lives; such as greater understanding of their children, help in sorting out their problems and a sense of 'regaining control and the ability to cope' (Shinman, 1994). The most significant cause of dissatisfaction was the length of waiting lists in some areas for a volunteer to be allocated.

• In 1992, the Department of Health funded a three-year project known as the Comprehensive Home-Start Initiative for Parental Support (CHIPS) which added four new schemes to an existing Home-Start programme in the borough of Wakefield. Researchers from Leeds University interviewed 46 of the 305 families being supported by the scheme at the start of their involvement and after six months (Frost et al., 1996). They found that two out of three mothers – including a high proportion with physical and mental health problems – had seen improvements in their emotional well-being. Among 35 families reporting behaviour management problems and other parenting difficulties, one in three said their involvement with Home-Start had helped them to make positive and consistent changes.[4]

- A study of family support work in two southern towns in the late 1980s reported that Home-Start's volunteers complemented the work of the statutory services. It found that volunteers were not only well-matched with the families they visited, but also able to work with a wide range of different needs (Gibbons and Thorpe, 1989)

- A study of 72 users and former users of Home-Start in the Midlands found that those who had been visited for some time were more positive about themselves and their ability to cope than new referrals. This was especially true of lone parents (Haynes, 1993).

- A four - year evaluation of the original Leicester scheme found families and referral agencies overwhelmingly convinced that visiting by Home-Start had brought change for the better. Volunteers interviewed were more hesitant in attributing change to their contribution. The study found that 86 per cent of the children visited who were on the 'at risk' register had remained out of care during the research period. It was not possible to attribute this with certainty to the role of Home-Start (Van der Eyken, 1982).

Funding and costs: the typical costs of establishing a Home-Start scheme, including volunteer training, are put at £37,000 in the first year and £34,000 in the second year. This includes an organiser's salary (in the range £12,915 to £15,624) and part-time secretarial help. The annual cost per family visited is approximately £500. Some Home-Start schemes have service agreements with social services, others receive funding from social services, health and, in some cases, education.

Comment: Home-Start is a good example of a service where trained volunteers can reinforce and add to the work of statutory agencies.

- It is evident that volunteers, often from similar social backgrounds to the families they are visiting, are an acceptable non-stigmatising way of reaching out to vulnerable families. According to the Audit Commission, this is a type of family support service that should be available in every local authority area (Audit Commission, 1994).

---

4.   Most of the families where there had been no improvement were continuing to receive support.

- Delinquency prevention is not among Home-Start's stated objectives, but it addresses a number of the known risk factors including parental supervision, harsh or inconsistent discipline and family conflict.

- In so far as it reduces the number of children taken in to care, it may be preventing both crime (in the form of child abuse) and criminality (in the sense that children in care run relatively high risks of later delinquency).

Pen Green Centre (Corby)

Brief description: the Pen Green Centre occupies a former school, complete with gymnasium. It opened in 1983 at a time when Corby was in deep economic difficulties following the closure of its steel works. It provides a wide range of support and educational services for children and parents for which it receives joint funding by education and social services. The centre has been used as a practice example by the Audit Commission (Audit Commission, 1994), is the subject of a book (Whalley, 1994) and features in a Foreign Office video – *Birth of a Nation*-on under-fives provision in the UK.

Location: the immediate neighbourhood served by the centre remains among the most socially disadvantaged in Northamptonshire. Local families using the centre include parents and children from a nearby hostel for homeless families.

Referrals: the centre keeps its doors open to the local community as a whole, not merely families referred there by social workers. As such it more closely resembles the 'open access' family centres run by voluntary organisations than those directly run by social services.

Programme: the main activities are:

- *Day nursery* – running since the centre opened, it has 39 full-time equivalent places of which half are offered to children deemed to be in need (including a few on the 'at risk' register) and half available on a first come, first served basis. A parent-run playgroup has been held at the centre for many years in response to a long waiting list for nursery places. The nursery curriculum developed at Pen Green, emphasising children's cognitive skills, has been favourably compared with that of High/Scope (see page 34), (Pugh et al., 1994). There is a strong commitment to parent involvement, beginning with a home visit by staff before children start. Staff have written their own assertiveness programme for under-fives, designed to raise children's self-confidence and make them less susceptible to bullying. 'Being safe', 'good touch, bad touch' and 'how to deal with strangers' are among the topics covered (Whalley, 1994).

- *Drop-in sessions* – Pen Green's open door to the local community is typified by the number of activities where parents are welcome whenever they choose to turn up. A family room has been set aside, with full-time worker, where parents can chat while their children play together. In addition, the main nursery facilities are made generally available for one morning a week and for an afternoon mother and toddler group. A weekly baby clinic run by a health visitor is another opportunity for parents to attend and be made aware of the centre's specialist services. In addition, there are 'messy' and other play sessions for toddlers that allow parents as well as children to socialise.

- *Older children* – the centre provides an out-of-school club for children aged 5–10 and a weekly evening youth club for 13- to 18-year olds.

- *Support groups* – the centre's specialist services include support groups for mothers-to-be, lone parents and parents of children with disabilities and other special needs. A men's group meets once a week, as does a group for women survivors of sexual abuse.

- *Parent education* – in addition to the groups already mentioned, two parent support groups are concerned with children's learning and ways they can be helped at home. There is a discussion and mutual support group for parents of teenagers. Women are offered an 'assertiveness through self-awareness' group. Parents wishing to learn more about child development, parenting and other issues meet weekly to study the Open University's 'Living in a Changing Society' course.

- *Further education and training* – the centre is home to government-funded adult literacy groups and to a 'Wider Opportunities' training programme for people who have been out of work for more than six months. Supported by the European Social Fund, the course includes vocational guidance, work placements and training. Those interested in working with children can work towards an NVQ in child care and education.

- *Home-Start* - Corby's Home-Start organisation (see page 13 above) is based at Pen Green and uses the centre to recruit and train parent volunteers.

Outcomes: no formal evaluation has been carried out at Pen Green. Staff monitoring suggests that the centre is currently used each week by:

- 400 families

- 65 children attending the day nursery (waiting list of over 100)

- 30 children x 9 'drop-in' playgroup sessions (some overlap)

- 200 individuals attending groups

- 40 primary school children using the after-school club

- 60 older children attending the youth club

- 25 adults on the 'Wider Opportunities' course.

Funding and costs: the core running costs of Pen Green Centre are £350,000 a year, divided equally between Northamptonshire's Social Services and Education Departments. Adult literacy work is government funded and the 'Wider Opportunities' course is funded by the European Social Fund. Money from the Single Regeneration Budget is currently being sought to expand the youth club activities.

The centre's multi-disciplinary staff include:

- Head of centre (social worker)

- Deputy head (teacher)

- 2 nursery teachers

- 7 family workers (NNEB or equivalent)

- Group work specialist (social worker)

- 2 employment and training co - ordinators ('Wider Opportunities')

- Home-Start coordinator

- Health visitors (weekly baby clinic)

- 2 part-time session workers

- Administrators and kitchen staff.

Comment: although no evaluation data is available on outcomes for different programmes used by families at Pen Green, the Audit Commission (Audit Commission, 1994) and others have described the centre as a model of good practice:

- the 'open access' policy draws in a large number of parents and children, including many vulnerable families, from a generally disadvantaged neighbourhood

- parents under stress who use the wide range of facilities can be drawn into the more specialist support groups without feeling stigmatised

- the centre is staffed by a multi-disciplinary team with joint funding from two local authority agencies.

In addition, it can be seen that:

- many of the family problems addressed by the centre are known 'risk factors' for children's later criminal involvement (notably parental supervision and discipline and children's educational under-achievement)

- the range of activities under the same roof, including Home-Start (see above), creates the 'one-stop shop' considered desirable by Crime Concern (Crime Concern, 1995) and others interested in the practicalities of criminality prevention programmes.

West Leeds Family Service Unit

Brief description: the Neighbourhood Centre, set up in West Leeds by the voluntary organisation Family Service Units, opened in 1989. Its aim is to relieve stress and to support parents and children in a socially disadvantaged area, making it less likely they will become involved with the statutory social services.

Location: the family centre uses a converted house in the multi-cultural Burley Lodges neighbourhood of Leeds.

Referrals: choosing to work as an 'open access' family centre, available to the local community as a whole, the project has resisted taking formal referrals of families whose children have been registered 'at risk'. Social services, health visitors and other agencies have been encouraged to recommend the project to individual families they believe would benefit from its services. However, it has recently been agreed that social services can refer up to 50 per cent of the participants in specialist, closed groups at the centre.

Programme: activities at the centre include 'drop in' sessions for mothers, money advice clinics, therapeutic group work for children, an anti-bullying programme, a play work in the home project and a holiday play scheme. Parents who make use of these services are made aware of more specialist groups which meet at the centre, including those for victims of domestic violence and for Asian or Afro-Caribbean women. In addition, there is a volunteer befriending scheme run for lone parents. The centre also operates an outreach advice centre and a women's group on a nearby estate.

Outcomes: an independent three-year evaluation by the University of Leeds Department of Adult Continuing Education found that just over half the adults using the project were Asian, 28 per cent were white and 19 per cent from other ethnic groups (Johnson, 1993). More than eight out of ten lived within a mile of the centre. Interviews with parents confirmed that the 'open door' policy meant they did not feel stigmatised by using the centre. Women (who accounted for the vast majority of users) had appreciated the opportunity to meet other families and make friends. They generally felt they had gained in confidence and self-esteem as a result of participating in the centre's activities. Some had used them as a stepping stone to training and further education courses. The available services and the support provided by staff and services were deemed especially helpful at times of family stress and participants felt that both they and their children had benefited. The researcher concluded that although the project had been less helpful to very withdrawn and sensitive women in the community, it had made a distinct contribution to preventing family breakdown.

Funding and costs: the centre's total budget for 1995–6 was £192,430 of which £148,206 related to staffing (equivalent 11 full-time posts). It received joint funding from Leeds Social Services Department and Leeds Health Authority with smaller grants from the Leeds Safer Cities initiative and charitable foundations.

Family Preservation

Child and Adolescent Psychiatry, Maudsley Hospital

Brief description: staff at the unit work with severely aggressive and disruptive children and their families who may lack even basic parenting skills. A clinical training programme, adapted from an American model (see

Forehand and McMahon, 1981), known as *The Parent-Child Game* has been in use for some years. Research has also begun on the potentially cost-effective use of group therapy for parents of conduct-disordered children using videotapes to model non-violent discipline and other techniques. This, too, is adapted from a well-established programme in the United States.

Location: the hospital is in Denmark Hill, South London.

Referrals: most families participating in the Parent-Child Game have been referred by social services. Parents taking part in the trials of group discussion and videotape modelling have children aged three to eight and have been referred to child psychiatric clinics in South London, Croydon and Chichester. The children who participated in a pilot programme displayed severe behavioural difficulties, but their parents were also found to be under serious stress – including high levels of unemployment, clinical depression and personality disorders.

Programmes: the Parent-Child Game is an innovative element that has been added to a more conventional process of individual and family case work for bringing the behaviour of conduct-disordered children within a 'normal' range. It places parents with their child in a video suite equipped with toys and games. The therapists observe them playing together through a one-way mirror and can speak to the parent through a microphone connected to an ear 'bug'. This allows the therapists to prompt the parent on ways to encourage and reward good behaviour while dealing effectively with disobedience or tantrums. During later sessions, the emphasis is on encouraging parents to give children clear commands and warnings and on praising them for their compliance (Gent, 1992).

The experimental training programme using videotapes consists of a 12-week course shown to groups of 10 to 12 adults led by a therapist. The videos (dubbed by English actors) comprise a series of 250 two-minute scenes in which children are seen interacting with parents in familiar situations. Each of these 'vignettes' is used to prompt reaction and discussion. The first part of the course focuses on encouraging pro-social activities, reading with children and spending time constructively. The second part is more directly concerned with reducing anti-social behaviour using non-violent discipline methods.

Outcomes: an unpublished pilot study of cases treated at the Maudsley using the Parent-Child Game suggests that improvements in children's behaviour are maintained for up to two years after treatment and that there is a high level of satisfaction with the training among parents (Whild, 1991). Although staff-intensive, the technique is considered effective in 'high risk' cases where the parent–child relationship is especially poor and where children's anti-social behaviour has reached an extreme (Gent, 1992).

A full trial of videotape training has begun, funded by the Department of Health. A total of 120 clinically referred parents will be divided into three- an experimental group who will follow the 3-month video course, a comparison group receiving conventional social work support and family therapy and a 'waiting list' control group of parents who will not take part in the video programme until the first courses have been completed. The evaluation will include questionnaires and 'before and after' video observation of parents and children interacting at home. A pilot study found a high level of uptake for the programme (fewer than 15 per cent of parents dropped out) and significant improvements in children's behaviour being maintained more than a year after the course. This accords with results for the American programme which achieved sustained improvements in the behaviour of parents and children. While a programme of one-to-one therapy with parents used 251 hours of staff time to achieve comparable results, the video discussion groups needed only 48 hours (Webster-Stratton, 1984).

Funding and costs: the clinical cost per family for treatment using the parent-child game is put at £600. The cost per family of a 12-week videotape course is estimated at £250. Neither figure includes research costs.

Family Nurturing Network

Brief description: the project makes use of two different course models developed in the United States. Both are aimed at families who are experiencing significant difficulties in parenting, including parents at risk of abusing or neglecting their children.

Location: Oxfordshire.

Referrals: most referrals are through health visitors and social workers.

Programmes: Family Nurturing Network offers two main programmes: *Family Connections* for parents and pre-school children, and the *Nurturing Programme* for parents and children aged 4–12. The former uses the same American video parenting programme being assessed at the Maudsley Hospital (see page 23 above). In Oxford, the course has been combined with play sessions suited to the needs of children, many of whom are found to be developmentally delayed. The nurturing programme for parents of older children concentrates on parental skills training and those aspects of family relationships that are most likely to reduce the risks of abuse. For example:

• personal responsibility and self-awareness

- understanding other people's feelings

- managing stress and anger

- the appropriate use of touch

- consistent, non-violent discipline

- assertiveness.

Groups of up to ten parents and 20 children attend for 15 weekly sessions of 2.5 hours each. Parents and children work in separate rooms on similar themes. The adults make use of handbooks, video scenes, discussions and role play, while the children take part in discussions, art sessions, games, play acting and music. There is a period of 'nurturing time' in each session when families get together for songs, games and a snack.

Outcomes: in 1995–6, the Network received 134 family referrals of whom 82 confirmed interest in the programme and 47 completed courses. The majority of families were living on low incomes and headed by a lone mother. There has been some success in attracting fathers to the project. Assessments of the course by parents, social workers and schools have been favourable (Utting, 1995; Quickenden, 1996). Internal evaluation of families before and after attending the *Family Connections* programme, using self-report and observational measures, suggests significant reductions in levels of parental anxiety and stress and significant improvements in self-esteem, relationships with children and child behaviour. An evaluation of the *Nurturing Programme* by a member of the Clinical Psychology Department at Exeter University, completed in 1996, compared outcomes for participating families with those of a control group who were waiting to take part in the programme. It found that the programme had led to significant improvements in parenting attitudes, emotional well-being and relationships with children. Children also felt more positive about their families by the end of the programme (Braffington, 1996). A one-year follow-up study of 121 abusing parents and 150 children who took part in a similar programme in the US found that 42 per cent had been discharged by social services, while seven per cent had been accused of further abuse (Bavolek, 1984)

Funding and costs: the average cost of taking a family through one of the courses is £1,800. This includes home assessment visits, liaison with referrers, training and volunteer expenses, programme materials and venue hire. The Family Nurturing Network was supported during a three year development phase by the Joseph Rowntree Foundation. It is now funded by Oxfordshire County Council and several charitable trusts.

Mellow Parenting

Brief description: like NEWPIN (see below), Mellow Parenting works with parents (mostly mothers) whose relationships with children are at or near the point of breakdown and whose own upbringing has often been marked by emotional, physical and sexual abuse and neglect. These and other personal preoccupations - such as current domestic violence - are addressed on an understanding that they are blocking the parents' ability to respond to the needs of their children.

Location: the programme has run for five years in family centres in Scotland's Central Region and a number of centres in south London including a psychiatric clinic at Guys Hospital. It is also being used in Sweden, Germany and Israel.

Referrals: referrals come from GPs, health visitors, social workers, child psychiatrists, educational psychologists and others working with families. Families who enter the project have to meet the referral criteria of either **one** of the following:

- a child on the protection register;

- persistent violence between adults;

- grave concern that the main caretaker has persistent difficulty in their relationships with a child

or **two** of the following:

- a child who has been showing signs of behavioural or emotional disorders for at least three months;

- a main caretaker with a mental disorder;

- a main caretaker with persistent relationship difficulties with their partner or family of origin;

- family living in social isolation, a violent neighbourhood and other environmental circumstances that place parents and children under stress.

Programme: Mellow Parenting's originators stress the importance of helping parents to find their own solutions to family management problems through mutual support and with a minimum of 'expert' guidance from professionals (Mills and Puckering, 1996). The programme runs for a full day each week for four months, combining personal group therapy and parent training using behaviour modification principles. The four main components are:

- videoing parents interacting with their children at home before they become part of a group. The group leader helps the parent to analyse what is happening. Parents 'own' the tapes and can choose which excerpts they wish to discuss with their group

- group work to explore parents' own childhood experiences and personal problems, making the link between these and relationships with their own children. Worksheets form the basis for discussion. (During this part of the day, children attend a crèche staffed by qualified care workers.)

- parenting education using video vignettes and personal examples to discuss practical problems. 'Homework' tasks are agreed for practice between sessions.

- a lunch and activity time bringing parents, children and staff together for play, games, arts and crafts, cooking, shopping and other shared events. Some of these sessions are also filmed for later discussion.

Parents who complete the programme are offered a short refresher course each summer.

Outcomes: a pilot evaluation of the first Mellow Parenting course at a family centre in Alloa found that 21 out of 28 mothers who began the programme had completed it (Puckering et al., 1994). Out of twelve children (six families) registered at risk of abuse at the start, ten had been removed from the register by the end of the programme and the remaining two were being supervised at home. This high level of de-registration compared with area figures showing fewer than a third of children being removed from the register each year. Coded observations, using 'before and after' videos, also showed significant improvements in parenting skills, including a substantial decline in instances of shouting, smacking and rough treatment. There were significant increases in parents offering their children physical affection, praise and stimulation. Parents reported improvements in their own self-confidence as well as their children's behaviour. A long-term follow-up study of Mellow Parenting is in progress, funded by the Department of Health.

Funding and costs: a Department of Health-funded study by the Centre for Economics of Mental Health, Institute of Psychiatry, comparing Mellow Parenting's cost effectiveness with other interventions available in family centres was due to be completed at the end of 1996. The major costs are those of two therapist/facilitators and two crèche workers for each session, plus meals, venue hire and equipment. Programmes have (variously) been funded by the National Health Service (clinical psychology), social services departments, Barnardos and the Aberlour Trust.

NEWPIN

Brief description: NEWPIN is a national voluntary agency helping parents under stress to break the cycle by which destructive family behaviour can be repeated from one generation to the next. It seeks to alleviate maternal depression and other mental distress while focusing on child-parent relationships and the prevention of emotional abuse. NEWPIN is cited in guidance to the Children Act as an example of services helping parents to feel less isolated, gain insight into their difficulties and to develop skills (Department of Health, 1991).

Location: NEWPIN was set up in south London in 1981 and is now active in 15 centres, including Chesterfield and Sheffield as well as London and the South East. Two centres are planned to open in Northern Ireland during 1997.

Referrals: parents who are socially isolated and experiencing difficulties in relationships with their children are referred to NEWPIN, chiefly by ante-natal clinics, psychiatrists, psychologists, health visitors and GPs. Self-referrals and referrals by existing members of NEWPIN are also accepted. Those referred are mothers (as main carers for their children), but fathers groups are being introduced following a pilot scheme.

Programme: after an extended home visit by the area coordinator, mothers choose whether to become involved in the project. Those that do are matched with a 'befriender' – an established user/member of the family centre who supports her until she has gained in confidence and begun to make her own friends. Once mothers become attached to the centre and their children are ready to be left in the playroom, they are invited to join a therapeutic support group. They may subsequently opt to take part in NEWPIN's Personal Development Programme (PDP) which consists of four components:

- parental skills training

- family play

- attachment and befriending

- preparation for work and further education (linked to NVQ training).

Together, the modules take just over a year to complete plus a further consolidation period of six months. Those who have completed the PDP may become befrienders, and include some who go on to train as NEWPIN coordinators.

Outcomes: an evaluation of NEWPIN funded by the Department of Health concluded that the emphasis on sharing and mutual support made it possible to provide intensive therapeutic services without creating dependency among mothers or a loss of self-respect (Cox et al., 1990; Pound, 1994). Women whose social deprivation and isolation made them unlikely candidates for conventional psychotherapy had used NEWPIN as a 'safe house' to explore themselves and their relationships with children. The study of 40 mothers found that the most significant improvements in mental state occurred among those who had the most sustained and intensive involvement with the programme. A different study of 214 parents referred to four of the longest-running centres during 1992, found that 46 per cent had made some use of NEWPIN, and 11 per cent were regular users, including eight per cent who had moved on to the PDP (Oakley et al., 1994). A sample of 93 mothers who returned a questionnaire included a third who made no use of NEWPIN after being referred. One in three said NEWPIN had helped with child-rearing problems, 17 per cent with 'not hurting their children' and seven per cent in preventing their children being taken into care. A further evaluation concerned with parenting skills and parent–child relationships was being planned at the time of writing.

Funding and costs: NEWPIN's national organisation is supported by the Department of Health and charitable trusts. Health and social services are the main funders of family centres. The 1995–6 budget for NEWPIN's Sheffield centre identified total running costs of £46,260 or which £31,960 relate to staffing. The budget for Deptford in south London was £68,500 of which salaries were £45,250. Organisers estimate the average cost of a

NEWPIN placement for one family at around £3,250 a year.

Radford Shared Care Project

Brief description: the project provides intensive assistance in the homes of families where children are believed to be at serious risk of neglect and abuse. Its aim is to improve parenting skills and children's life chances to a point where care proceedings no longer need be contemplated.

Location: NCH–Action for Children and Nottinghamshire County Council launched the project as a partnership in the Radford area of Nottingham in 1989. Its catchment area has since been expanded.

Referrals: families offered the service are clients of the social services and include children considered at high risk of being accommodated by the local authority. The project began as a response to four mothers who were pregnant and who – because they had already had children removed into care – risked having their babies taken away from them. The project now works with the families of children of all ages whose difficulties stem from poor parental nurturing and control and inadequate stimulation.

Programme: in addition to support from local authority social workers, each family receives up to four hours a week help in the home from a team of five trained 'shared care workers'. The workers are experienced in child - care and come from multi-ethnic backgrounds. Their role is to form a working relationship with parents, while modelling basic parenting skills including play and stimulation and the use of consistent, non-violent discipline. It is considered important to address parents' own needs as well as the relationship with their children, encouraging them to gain confidence and work out their own answers to parenting problems. The project includes supporting group work for mothers and – in recent months – for fathers as well.

Outcomes: the project works with 15 families at any one time but may have dealings with over 30 families in a full year. One target is to keep children safe from abuse and to ensure that at least 80 per cent remain living at home. An evaluation by Nottingham University of the project's first two years found that none of the 50 children being supervised within 28 families had been taken into care. In subsequent years between 80 per cent and 92 per cent of children have been retained safely at home. The shared care workers were deemed to have been successful in building on the existing strengths of the parents they worked with and their intervention was, in many cases, regarded as positive and helpful.(Fleming and Ward, 1992). Further research has concluded there is good evidence for the project meeting its objectives and that "in many cases project workers have had a profound impact on families"(Butler, 1994 - 6).

Funding and costs: the total cost of the programme for 1995–6 was £94,200 (including research, premises and depreciation) of which £74,600 was attributable to staffing. The programme is 65 per cent funded by Nottinghamshire County Council and 35 per cent by NCH–Action for Children.

Young Offender Community Support Scheme

Brief description: by placing young offenders with specially recruited foster families, the project's immediate object is to prevent the need for 15-

to 21- year-olds to be remanded into secure accommodation or custody or to be given a custodial sentence. It views custody as a negative experience, likely to accelerate criminal careers and undermine the potential for personal and social responsibility. By giving young offenders security in a stable, family home the aim is to help them tackle their criminal behaviour and make constructive plans for the future.

Location: Hampshire (including a bail remand pilot scheme in the north of the county only).

Referrals: the young offenders taking part are clients of the Probation and Youth Justice services.

Programme: the programme recruits and pays support families to care for young offenders on placements of up to a year. After assessment, the foster parent(s) receive special training and are expected to guide young people towards a more routine, self-disciplined way of life. They encourage them to search for work, training or education and to make constructive use of their leisure time. Families are supported by regular home visits from the project staff, who make themselves available by telephone out of hours. The project is divided between a programme for young offenders and a bail scheme for young people who would otherwise be remanded to a children's home, secure accommodation or custody. Plans are being considered for an expansion of the scheme from March 1997 as part of a comprehensive bail remand strategy for the county.

Monitoring and evaluation: an external evaluation by the Dartington Social Research Unit two years after the project started found it had uncovered a 'rich seam' of foster families prepared to take in and shelter young people whom others had abandoned. The 21 young offenders placed were recidivists marked by the persistence rather than the severity of their criminal behaviour. All had disrupted family backgrounds and all but five had previously been in local authority care. Eight remained in their foster placement until its planned conclusion, but 13 left prematurely. In the 10 to 18 months following placement there were 13 who committed further offences, but the rate of reoffending was reduced. All but one of the seven who maintained a clean record had remained in the project's care for at least six months. Taken with evidence of progress with self-esteem, personal skills, job training and employment, the researchers concluded that the scheme had established a valuable new model.(Dartington Social Research Unit, 1993).

Subsequent monitoring has confirmed that the longer young people are able to remain with their foster families, the greater the chance of successful outcomes. Some 75 per cent of those placed on the scheme between 1993 and 1995 either committed no further offences or significantly reduced their rate of offending.

Funding and costs: the project's budget for 1994–5 was £131,400, including £67,600 staffing costs and £39,000 in allowances paid to foster parents. It was funded by £58,400 from Hampshire Probation Service and Hampshire Social Services Department, £29,200 from NCH-Action for Children and £43,800 from other charitable grants.

Community Placement Scheme - South Glamorgan

Since the early 1980s, Social Services in South Glamorgan have run a Community Placement Scheme, providing 35 places in foster families for young people aged 10 to 18 involved in serious or persistent offending or who exhibit seriously challenging behaviour. In 1987, the Youth Justice section introduced a Remand Fostering Scheme for young people who were unable to return home. The costs per child were estimated at £311 per week (South Glamorgan Social Services Department, 1995).

3. Schools

Introduction

In the past 20 years there has been growing recognition of the part that formal education can play in reducing the chances that children will turn to crime. It is now acknowledged that the family and the school are two socialising institutions that, taken together, can either make or break a criminal career (Graham and Utting, 1996).

The programmes selected for inclusion in this chapter address important school-based risk factors identified by research. These are:

• low educational achievement

• troublesome and disruptive behaviour in school

• bullying behaviour

• persistent truancy

• permanent exclusion from school.

Projects have the primary aim of improving children's educational attainment and behaviour in school, but in so doing they will also influence criminality. Research has shown that schools have an independent part to play, in addition to families, in socialising children and reducing the risks of delinquency (Graham, 1988).

The programmes described in this chapter address the relevant risk factors by focusing on individual pupils or on the overall organisation and ethos of schools. In practice, it is a combination of these two approaches that is required. The value of adopting a 'whole school' strategy to tackle problems such as bullying, truancy and disruptive behaviour is now widely recognised in Britain.

One ingredient of a whole-school approach that makes an important connection between this and the previous chapter on families is the importance of co - operation between schools and parents (Pilling, 1990). One of the most significant protective factors found in the backgrounds of children from disadvantaged homes whose attainment is above average is having a parent who displays a keen interest in their education. Persistent truancy has also been linked to parental attitudes to school and levels of education (MVA Consultancy, 1991).

Parental support increases the chances that children will become attached to their schools and committed to learning. However, it is also to be expected that the increased risks of anti-social behaviour among children who lack a supportive family, can be mitigated by a commitment to school and the pro-social values that it promotes (Maughan, 1994). UK programmes in which the importance of home–school links is stressed include the DfEE's current anti-bullying campaign and projects funded under *Truancy and Disaffected Pupils GEST* initiative.

The projects described in this chapter overlap considerably. For the sake of presentation, they are categorised as :

• Raising school attainment

  High/Scope UK

• Preventing exclusions and truancy:

  Cities in Schools (UK)

  Dorset Health Alliance Project

  Truancy and Disaffected Pupils GEST Programme

• Preventing Bullying

  Anti-bullying Initiative (Merseyside and London)

  Sheffield Anti-Bullying Initiative

• Crime and anti-social behaviour awareness

  Education and Prevention of Crime (EPOC)

  Schools Crime Awareness and Reduction Programme (SCARP)

Raising school attainment

High/Scope UK

Brief description: the pre-school curriculum and approach to learning devised by the High/Scope Educational Research Foundation in Michigan, USA has gained a considerable foothold in the United Kingdom in recent years. British interest in this (as opposed to other well-defined, cognitive curricula) is largely due to the impressive results that have emerged from longitudinal research conducted by the parent organisation in America. This not only ascribes significant educational benefits to the programme, but also a positive effect in reducing criminality (see below). Investment in quality pre-school education can, on the basis of the High/Scope research, be portrayed as a cost-effective use of public money.

Location: it is estimated that more than 42,000 children a year attend nursery schools, playgroups and other pre-school settings in Britain using the High/Scope programme (High/Scope UK 1995; Pirani, 1994). Nursery classes provided by Hertfordshire County Council, for example, are run on High/Scope lines, while the Home Office Programme Development Unit (PDU) has supported the introduction of nurseries in North Tyneside, Lewisham, Manchester and Liverpool.

Programme: the High/Scope approach is one of 'child initiated learning' where pre-school children are encouraged to make positive choices about the play activities they wish to pursue (Schweinhart et al., 1986) A 'plan-do-review' process is used during each session to help children make their decisions and think about the way they put them into effect. Staff are trained to recognise and make use of learning opportunities that arise spontaneously during play ('key experiences'). To achieve this, a ratio of at least one teacher to 10 children is recommended with a maximum class size of 20. The routine structure of each session incorporates such features as a 'greeting circle', small group activities, tidy up time, outside play time, snack time and story time. The organisation of the classroom is considered important so that all the play items are within reach of small children and can be found (and put away) in their allocated space. Close contact with parents is encouraged as a way of ensuring that learning activities and experiences are reinforced in the home. Home visiting was a feature of the early American model, but not one included in the projects which the PDU supported in Britain.

Outcomes: monitoring data for the four 'Young Children First' projects funded by the PDU is being assembled. The main objectives of these programmes, sited in areas with long-term problems of crime and criminality, are:

- the promotion of positive self image and independent learning skills

- a confident and competent transition to school

- parental involvement in children's learning to produce a longer term supportive role to their children.

An evaluation of this project by the University of Newcastle is – inevitably given the time-scale – concerned with these issues rather than the ability or otherwise of High/Scope to reduce criminality. The most convincing evidence of its value in criminality reduction continues to be the long-term outcomes of the Perry Pre-School Programme, which was launched more than 30 years ago in a disadvantaged, black neighbourhood of Ypsilanti, Michigan. The programme randomly assigned matched pairs among more than 120 children aged three and four to a control group or to an experimental group who were given a quality pre-school experience for up to two years. The latter attended class for 2.5 hours a day for 30 weeks a year. Each family received a weekly home visit of 1.5 hours. The pupil–teacher ratio was even higher than that now recommended by High/Scope. The parents of the children were notable for their low socio-economic status, poor employment records and limited educational attainment. Homes tended to be overcrowded and half the families were headed by a lone parent (Schweinhart et al., 1993). The primary aim of the pre-school enrichment experiment was to see if educational underachievement among high risk children could be redressed. In so doing it was also hoped that better school performance would improve employment prospects and reduce the risks of delinquency. Educational attainment and other aspects of the children's lives were monitored through to young adulthood. By the age of 19, it was apparent that, compared with the control group, those who had attended pre-school were:

- less likely to have needed special educational support

- more likely to have completed their schooling (high school graduation)

- more likely to have found a job

- less likely (in the case of girls) to have become pregnant

- less likely to have been arrested (arrest rates were 40 per cent lower) (Berrueta-Clement et al., 1984).

By the age of 27, the experimental group were:

• more likely to have earnings over $2,000 per month

• more likely to own their own homes

• less likely to have needed social services in the past 10 years

• less likely to have been arrested (and especially to have been arrested five or more times)

• Less likely to have been arrested for drug-related offences (Schweinhart et al., 1993).

In venturing an explanation as to why a comparatively short pre-school intervention could have had this long-term influence, the High/Scope researchers used their longitudinal data to trace a causal pathway. They argued that improved intellectual performance in early childhood led to greater motivation in elementary school which reduced the need for special education and increased the likelihood of completing their education. Higher educational performance was, in turn, associated with fewer arrests and better job prospects. Specifically, they related their results to the curriculum encouragement given to initiative, responsibility for actions, curiosity, independence and self-confidence in small children. Support for this view comes from research comparing outcomes from High/Scope's curriculum with those of a highly tutored 'direct instruction' class and the child-initiated play of a more conventional nursery school. All three achieved improvements in children's IQ, but by age 23 children who had attended the pre-school classes where they had chosen their own activities had only a third of the arrests recorded for the direct instruction group (Schweinhart and Weikart, forthcoming).

Funding and costs: Home Office funding via the PDU for the four experimental High/Scope nurseries has been £165,000 over three years. It is difficult to specify the cost of setting up a High/Scope programme in the UK, since the curriculum is marketed as a training package for those working in the early years sector who already have an initial qualification. The facilities in which they work may already be well established and require little investment to be reorganised on High/Scope lines. The current cost for training nursery staff with an additional small investment in materials is around £5,000. Training in Britain is provided by High/Scope Institute staff and over 100 'endorsed trainers' around the country. Over 1,000 practitioners have successfully completed the curriculum implementation course allowing them to claim High/Scope accreditation.

In the United States, it is acknowledged that the recommended ratio of children to staff makes the curriculum more expensive to implement than many of the 'Headstart' pre-school programmes funded by the Federal government. Nevertheless, it has been calculated that for every $1 originally invested in the Perry Pre-School Programme, there has been a return to the taxpayer – in reduced crime, lower demand for special education, welfare and other public services – of over $7 in real terms (Barnett, 1993).

Comment: the results of the Perry Pre-School Programme are impressive, but need to be cited with care in the UK context (Graham and Bennett, 1995). Even in the most disadvantaged neighbourhoods, the circumstances of children under-5 in Britain are different to those of an impoverished, urban black community in early 1960s America. It might be unrealistic to expect such striking results in terms of criminality reduction, from pre-school programmes in the UK (see Woodhead, 1985). Moreover, although the Perry research associates the long-term results with the quality of pre-school experience, it does not follow that the High/Scope curriculum is the *only* quality curriculum that can lead to desirable long-term effects (Osborn and Millbank, 1987). The evidence that pre-school education of a high quality has the potential to reduce criminality, nevertheless, creates a powerful adjunct to the educational case established by both British and American research (Sylva, 1994; Lazar and Dartington, 1982).

Preventing Exclusions and truancy

Cities in Schools

Brief description: teaching for children excluded from schools has tended to be concentrated in off-site units that carry the stigma of being 'sin bins' for disruptive pupils. Cities in Schools (UK) has devised a *Bridge Course* allowing teenagers whose secondary education has broken down to pursue further education and work experience in mainstream settings. It is also responsible for programmes designed to reintegrate younger children who have been permanently excluded into schools and various preventive interventions. The organisation specifies crime reduction among its objectives.

Location: in the past three years, 75 projects have been established across the UK in Cardiff, London, Liverpool and other urban areas and in rural areas including Cambridgeshire, Norfolk and the Vale of Glamorgan. A number of authorities are applying the complete Cities in Schools strategy of *Bridge*, *Reintegration* and *Prevention* courses.

Referrals: young people aged 14 to 19 can be referred to the *Bridge Course* if there is no appropriate school for which they are eligible or if they are outside education, training or employment. Participants include persistent non-attenders, excluded pupils and young people awaiting court hearings or subject to court supervision orders. The primary target for reintegration projects is permanently excluded pupils aged 8 to 14.

Programme: *Bridge Course* – groups of ten young people are placed under the supervision of a personal tutor or 'mentor' while they attend a weekly study programme at a further education college, take part in work experience with local employers and pursue a life skills and personal development course. Tutors are expected to maintain close liaison with the young people's families and/or carers. The curriculum framework is broadly based, but emphasises literacy, numeracy, computer awareness and communication skills. It can be accredited through National Record of Achievement (NRA), National Vocational Qualification (NVQ) or the Youth Award Scheme. Local schemes are run as separately constituted charities with boards that seek a partnership between education, social services, the police, Training and Enterprise Councils, private business and local leaders.

Reintegration Course – pupils who are long-term non-attenders or have been permanently excluded are involved in an intensive six-week programme of assessment and individual supervision which may include anger management and other therapies as well as teaching and help in pursuing constructive leisure activities (minimum 15 hours a week contact time). They are then reintegrated into a new school with course tutors providing supervision that ranges, as required, from full-time support in class to occasional help with homework plus a weekly tutorial. The process is completed by a further six - week period when the extra supervision is progressively removed and the pupil's progress is monitored.

Prevention programmes – Cities in Schools has worked with schools in disadvantaged areas of Cardiff and the London Borough of Brent to tackle aggressive behaviour and truancy. A strong emphasis on encouraging home–school links includes training for staff in behaviour management and on working in partnership with parents. Schools have also been helped to draw up 'whole school' policies on bullying and other behavioural issues.

Outcomes: of the young people who participated in *Bridge Courses* during 1994–5, more than 40 per cent were known to the police (rising to 100 per cent in one Cambridgeshire project). Monitoring of students in Gwent, South Glamorgan, Cambridgeshire and Liverpool showed they had achieved an average attendance level of over 80 per cent. This was a marked improvement on previous school attendance (a 100 per cent improvement for one group in Gwent). Nearly all those eligible achieved their National Record of Achievement. The immediate outcomes for three out of four students were known to be positive, including almost a third going on to further education and a quarter to youth training. Commenting on *Bridge Courses* in the context of truancy prevention, an independent evaluation team reporting to the DfEE concluded that they constituted 'a very important model for the future' because of their ability to reconnect disaffected young people with the education system (Learmonth, 1995) The target set for the reintegration courses is that 80 per cent of excluded children should be returned to the mainstream schooling system.

Funding and costs: the inclusive cost of a *Bridge Course* for ten students is between £45,000 and £50,000 a year. Cities in Schools suggest that this compares favourably with the annual costs of off-site pupil referral units (PRUs) or home tuition of between £8,000 and £16,000 per head respectively. The cost of the reintegration courses is estimated at between £6,000 and £7,000 a year per pupil. In addition to local education authorities and social services, funding for some courses has been obtained through the Department for Education and Employment's *Grants for Education Support and Training (GEST)* initiative (see below), Training and Enterprise Councils, the European Union, the Single Regeneration Budget, private companies and individual schools. The DfEE's independent evaluation of truancy reduction programmes concluded that *Bridge Courses* offered good value for money compared with placements in off-site PRUs (Learmonth, 1995).

Dorset Health Alliance Project

Brief description: this experimental project, which was sponsored by the Home Office Programme Development Unit, was concerned with the relationship between children's education, health and anti-social criminal behaviour. It promoted closer parent–school links while tackling a range of behavioural problems, including disruptive behaviour, truancy and bullying.

Location: a disadvantaged estate on the edge of Bournemouth.

Referrals: an experienced education social worker was based at the local primary school, working with children and their families. His work with children continued after they had moved up to the neighbourhood secondary school. Working with the social worker were two project teachers (one full-time in primary school and one part-time in secondary school).

Programmes: The project launched a number of inter-related initiatives including:

• home visits to encourage attendance at school parents' evenings

- establishing home-school contact with families of vulnerable children (including those who had shown poor health and development in pre-school tests)

- anti-bullying campaigns, including use of the non-judgemental, non-punitive technique known as 'shared concern' for persuading suspected bullies to desist

- preventing exclusions and truancy by enlisting the active support of parents in setting targets for pupils to improve their behaviour

- family therapy with the families of pupils with serious behaviour problems and dysfunctional homes

- an after-school club for up to 16 primary school pupils

- training in assertiveness and other social skills for sixth year primary school pupils

- health education for seventh and eighth year pupils, addressing family life and sexual responsibility issues.

In addition, the social worker played a more conventional co - ordinating role in organising support for children at risk of abuse and for families under stress.

Outcomes: an evaluation report by Prof. Colin Pritchard of Southampton University for the Home Office PDU was in preparation at the time of writing.

Funding and costs: the project received a Home Office PDU grant of £225,000 over three years plus £20,000 from Dorset County Council. The costs included evaluation.

Truancy and Disaffected Pupils GEST Programme

Brief description: the Department for Education and Employment, under its Grants for Education Support and Training (GEST) programme, has given priority to a wide range of initiatives intended to reduce levels of truancy and disaffection among pupils. Some of the money, channelled through LEAs, has funded projects described under separate headings in this report (for example, *Cities in Schools* and *Parent Network*). This section provides an overview of the 'TDP GEST' programme as summarised in an independent evaluation commissioned by the DfEE (Learmonth, 1995).

Location: GEST funding was provided for 71 truancy reduction projects in English LEAs in 1993–4 and 85 projects in 1994–5, including 43 'Truancy Watch' programmes.

Referrals: the aim of the overall programme was to improve levels of attendance for children of compulsory school age at designated schools with poor attendance records or particular problems with post-registration truancy and to improve the provision for disaffected pupils.

Programmes: the range of projects can be summarised as:

• Better registration procedures. Attempts to introduce more systematic procedures for registration and following-up on non-attenders included experiments with information technology (notably the use of computerised swipe cards for registration). It was suggested that most schools make insufficient use of available data about non-attenders when shaping their policies and practices (Learmonth, 1995).

• Action on the first day of absence. A substantial share of TDP GEST funding went to development and training projects involving the Educational Welfare Service. These included the use of Educational Welfare Officers and trained Educational Welfare Assistants to make contact with families from the first day that a pupil's unauthorised absence from school is confirmed. A pilot project in Dorset trained young people in their late teens and early 20s to befriend and mentor persistent truants, encouraging their regular attendance at school.

• Parent support and education. Many LEAs used leaflets that advised parents what they could do to ensure their children attended school regularly. Others went further, arranging mutual support meetings for parents of young truants and, in some cases, offering parenting education. A *Parent-Link* course funded by TDP GEST ran in Bedfordshire[1] while a Newcastle primary school worked with Save the Children to offer multi-agency support to parents as well as 'positive parenting' classes (Learmonth, 1995) The latter included the appointment, one-day a week, of a support teacher to help junior school pupils with poor attendance records and attainment to make the otherwise difficult transition to secondary school.[2]

• Anti-bullying. GEST funds helped schools to develop 'whole school' anti-bullying strategies. The section on the *Sheffield Anti-Bullying Initiative* (see below, page 47) describes this important approach in more detail.

---

1. See Parent Network in Chapter 2 of this report.
2. The Home Office PDU-funded Dorset Health Alliance project described in this report has also been concerned with the trasition from primary to secondary schools.

- Stronger pastoral support. Better personal support for pupils and efforts to improve their social skills was seen as a way of preventing disaffection and increasing their participation in school. Examples included the use in Dudley primary schools of certificates and badges for pupils who improved their attendance and 'quality circles' where pupils were encouraged to listen to each other and offer understanding and mutual support.

- Work with 'hard core' truants. A range of schemes used vocational training and work experience as a means of regaining the interest of persistent secondary school non-attenders in education. In addition to *Cities in Schools* Bridge Courses (see above) the GEST-funded projects included a School time and Enterprise Programme (STEP) in East Sussex which offered tailor-made work placements for one day a week as part of a contract requiring improved school attendance, signed by young people and their parents.

- Truancy Watch. Based on a pilot scheme in Stoke on Trent, Truancy Watch schemes were introduced to engage wider, community support in identifying and reporting truants. They included the nomination of 'truancy-free zones' in shopping centres, referral 'hotlines' and patrols. This was subsequently modified in many areas to emphasise the vulnerability of young people out of school in terms of missed schooling and as potential victims of crime.

- Behaviour management training for staff. Some schools and LEAs organised training for teachers and playground supervisors in techniques for encouraging good behaviour and dealing consistently with misbehaviour. Courses addressed ways of tackling pupil disaffection and underachievement.

- Curriculum improvements. The curriculum and the way it is taught can both influence attendance. Some schools received GEST funding to provide remedial teaching in reading, arithmetic and other basic skills and to introduce training in assertiveness and other social skills. There were also initiatives to introduce more vocational training in secondary schools.

The whole-school approach recommended by the DfEE to address bullying (see *The Sheffield Anti-Bullying Initiative*, page 47 below) was also applied to improving attendance. It required a school attendance policy to be drawn up, based on a detailed assessment of registration and other available data.

Outcomes: the DfEE's independent evaluation of schemes found little hard data as to the impact of TDP GEST on juvenile crime rates. In the context of

'Truancy Watch', it noted local assessments suggesting very little shopping centre crime was attributable to children absent without authority from school. It, nevertheless, concluded there was ample evidence that schools could influence attendance and tackle disaffection among their pupils. Although there was no quick or simple way of tackling truancy, the evaluation identified a number of lessons for schools and LEAs anxious to improve their performance:

- In the short-term, a same day response to unauthorised absence, including contact with parents, can improve attendance rates by 5 to 10 per cent – although it has little effect on hard-core non attendance.

- In the medium term, a planned, whole-school approach based on a detailed understanding of the problems in individual schools, will have the most substantial impact on attendance rates. Whole-school approaches are the only effective way to tackle post-registration truancy.

- The quality of planning, training and analysis of relevant data is crucial in determining whether investment in anti-truancy measures is cost-effective and accepted by pupils, their families and staff.

- The most efficient and effective interventions in terms of value for money are those which work preventively before hard-core absenteeism develops. In dealing with persistent truants curriculum initiatives such as the *Cities in Schools* Bridge Courses (see above) are a less expensive means of reconnecting non-attenders with the education system than 'off-site' Pupil Referral Units.

Funding and costs: GEST provided £9.6 million for truancy reduction programmes in 1993–4 and £14 million for truancy and disaffected pupils programmes in 1994–5. Grants covered 60 per cent of the cost of projects with the remaining 40 per cent provided by local education authorities.

Preventing bullying

The Sheffield Anti-Bullying Initiative

Brief description: bullying has been broadly defined as a "the repeated oppression of a less powerful person by a more powerful one" (Farrington, 1993). It applies to a range of behaviour that extends from persistent name-calling and telling nasty stories behind the victim's back to activities such as theft, extortion and physical assault that are treated in the adult world as criminal. The 1989 Elton report on school discipline described bullying as a widespread problem that tended to be ignored by teachers (Dept. of Education and Science/Welsh Office, 1989). The anti-bullying initiative which the Department for Education supported in Sheffield demonstrates how schools can exert an effective influence over anti-social behaviour among pupils. The lessons learned through a three-year research programme have been made available to all state schools.(Sharp and Smith, 1994) The DfEE's current anti-bullying campaign (Department for Education, 1994)., which urges schools to adopt a whole - school policy, is substantially derived from this project. It has also been determined that registered school inspectors should seek the views of pupils, parents and teachers on the incidence of bullying and the school's response (Dept. for Education, 1994).

Location: twenty three primary and secondary schools in Sheffield.

Programme: a 1990 survey of over 6,700 pupils in Sheffield (Smith and Sharp, 1994) found that:

- one in four primary school children (27 per cent) and one in ten secondary school pupils (10 per cent) said they had been bullied at some time during the preceding term

- one in ten primary school children (10 per cent) and one in 25 in secondary schools (4 per cent) said they were bullied once a week or more often

- one in eight primary school children (12 per cent) and one in 14 secondary pupils admitted to sometimes taking part in bullying.

On the basis of previous anti-bullying programmes, especially those in Norway, the 23 participating schools were encouraged to take a whole - school approach. Instead of focusing the initiative on individual bullies or their victims, this required them to seek the support of all those associated with the school – governors, staff, parents and pupils – for a clear and enforceable policy. Consultation and implementation were accompanied by systematic monitoring, evaluation and review.

A whole - school policy on bullying would typically include:

- a statement of aims and objectives

- a definition of unacceptable 'bullying' behaviour

- an account of the preventive steps being taken

- a description of the disciplinary procedures to be followed when bullying occurred.

Schools were also given the option of introducing other measures designed to reinforce the core policy. These included:

- anti-bullying material as part of the curriculum (using, for example, videos, plays and stories to raise awareness)

- teaching problem-solving skills (the idea of encouraging small groups of pupils to analyse bullying problems and develop solutions in 'quality circles' was borrowed from industry)

- assertiveness training to increase self-confidence (offered to victims of bullying or, sometimes, whole classes)

- innovative methods for dealing with bullies (staff training was made available in 'shared concern' and other 'no blame' techniques where pupils suspected of bullying are told about their victim's problems and asked to help in resolving them)

- peer counselling (two secondary schools trained interested pupils in listening and other skills before establishing them as a point of contact for those being bullied)

- better playground supervision (the role and status of lunchtime supervisors was given greater recognition, supported by training in behaviour management techniques)

- environmental improvements (schools identified and tackled the bullying 'hot spots' on their sites, such as boring, featureless playgrounds, long corridors and a lack of lunchtime activities.

Outcomes. detailed research, including a follow-up survey carried out in 1993, suggested that the interventions had a positive impact on bullying (Smith and Sharp, 1994). But there were wide differences between schools with evidence that those who put more effort into anti-bullying strategies generally achieved better results. Specifically:

- the project schools showed a statistically significant increase in the proportion of pupils saying they had not been bullied and a significant decrease in the reported frequency of bullying. These effects were most marked in primary schools.

- although five out of seven secondary schools showed some increase in the number of pupils saying they had not been bullied that term, the average was weighted in the opposite direction by one school where substantially more bullying was reported than three years earlier.

- a significant increase in the proportion of pupils saying they would not join in bullying was more marked in secondary schools than in primary schools.

- an increase in pupils' willingness to tell teachers if they were bullied was modest in primary schools, but substantial in secondary schools.

There is reason to believe that these results are an underestimate of what was actually achieved. As the researchers point out, the detailed attention given to the subject is likely to have made pupils more conscious of bullying and more likely to remember incidents of being bullied. Results from playground monitoring and from detailed, qualitative interviews with pupils also suggested that the amount of change is under-represented by the main survey. There was additional evidence that bullying problems may have generally worsened over the same period in other Sheffield schools (Whitney et al., 1994).

Comment: the main reasons for challenging bullying behaviour cited in the DfEE pack for schools are:

- the safety and happiness of pupils

- educational achievement – bullying can disrupt the victim's learning and, in extreme cases, lead to truancy

- providing children with a model for helpful behaviour and a clear definition of what is unacceptable

- improving the school's reputation as effective and caring.

In addition, however, there is the opportunity to tackle the increased risks that school bullies will grow into aggressive and violent young adults, compared with other children (Olweus, 1991).

The work done in Sheffield (and in similar work introduced as part of the *Safer Cities* initiative in Wolverhampton[3]) has created models of 'good practice' which schools can apply with confidence. The initiative also provides a practical demonstration of ways that governors, staff, parents and pupils can work together to raise standards of education and behaviour. Research suggests that this whole - school approach has an important part to play in tackling other risk factors associated with delinquency.

---

3. Wolverhampton schools are featured in the DfE training video *Bullying: don't suffer in silence.*

Anti-Bullying Initiative (Merseyside and London)

Brief description: similar messages to those emerging from the Sheffield programme can be found in the evaluation of an anti-bullying initiative sponsored by the Home Office in four contrasted schools. In particular, the researchers conclude that simultaneous change in both the physical and social environment of a school is necessary if individual and group behaviour is to alter significantly (Pitts and Smith, 1995).

Location: Merseyside and London (one primary and one secondary school in each).

Programme: a 1991 survey of pupils found that bullying was most frequent in the two primary schools and that it declined as pupils moved up through secondary schools. Name-calling was the most common form of victimisation, but as many as half the primary pupils and one in four secondary pupils reported being hit or kicked. Racial taunts and insults against pupils' families ('cussing') were more common in the London schools, which both had significant ethnic minority populations (Pitts and Smith, 1995). The London secondary school, in Tower Hamlets, was notable for high levels of racial tension and general turbulence among pupils. Although not described as a whole - school strategy, the 'organisational development' approach adopted was concerned with gaining the support of pupils and staff at all levels and reflecting their interests and needs. Work, including the production of an anti-bullying code of practice and an implementation strategy, was tailored to each school's needs. The London primary school used improvised drama and discussion to raise bullying issues and involved staff and pupils in making a video explaining the school's new anti-bullying policy. The Merseyside primary school included a programme of peer education in which older pupils talked to younger ones about their views of bullying and how to deal with it. The Merseyside secondary school introduced an eight-session 'Assertiveness and Empowerment' course into the Personal and Social Education curriculum. The London secondary school adopted a range of strategies including a survey of poorly supervised sites and the inclusion of bullying-related issues in the curriculum.

Evaluation: the programmes in both primary schools recorded significant improvements between 1991 and 1993 in the proportion of pupils reporting they had not been bullied in the past three months. In the London school, this appeared to reflect a different perception of the way teachers and other staff would respond to reports of bullying. On Merseyside the connection seemed to be with the pupil-led initiative to ensure that bullying incidents were reported (Pitts and Smith, 1995). The Merseyside secondary school also achieved a significant reduction in the reported level of bullying, but–in spite of considerable efforts by pupils and staff – no such change occurred in the London school. The researchers point out that the follow-up survey took place at a time of heightened racial tension and gang violence in Tower Hamlets following the election of a British National Party local councillor. There was evidence of a significant decline in violent bullying among younger pupils (Year 7), although not in the school overall.

Crime and anti-social behaviour awareness

Education and Prevention of Crime (EPOC)

Brief description: wide-ranging programmes of multi-disciplinary youth activities aimed at reducing juvenile crime were initiated by the National Association for the Care and Resettlement of Offenders (NACRO) in four secondary schools. Although inconclusive as to its effects on the incidence of youth crime and truancy, the three-year initiative, sponsored by the Department for Education, confirmed the potential value of schools as a base for multi-agency work with young people.

Location: an (unidentified) secondary school in each of four different urban areas took part between 1990 and 1993. The areas were all characterised by social disadvantage and evidence of a youth crime problem.

Referrals: the programmes of activities were available to all pupils. A decision was taken not to target individuals.

Programmes: three of the four pilot schools established a multi-disciplinary 'Youth Affairs Group' whose members included teaching staff, educational welfare officers, careers officers, social workers, youth workers and the police. A questionnaire survey of pupils was used to help plan a programme of in- and out-of-school activities intended to 'promote more positive relationships between young people and their communities'. These included:

In-School	**Out-of-school**
Anti-bullying project	Environmental improvements;
Drop-in counselling and advice	Outdoor pursuits (including Duke
Youth forum (school council)	of Edinburgh's Award Scheme)
Crime prevention meetings	Young leaders' programme
Sport/drama activities (after-school	Drama and dance sessions
and during holidays);	Soccer school
Youth worker in school	Girls' group.
Detached youth worker.	

Outcomes: an unpublished evaluation by David Galloway and Mike Smith of Durham University for the Home Office found that although a majority of young people taking part in EPOC activities did not have a criminal record, the proportion of known offenders who participated was similar to that for non-offenders. It was impossible to prove that EPOC had led to a reduction in delinquency or related problems such as truancy and exclusion. This was partly due to difficulties in assembling comparable statistics from the police. One police authority did provide figures which suggested that an EPOC school had achieved a more sustained, year-on-year reduction in the proportion of known offenders between 1990 and 1993 than other schools in the same area. However, the fall in delinquency was not maintained in 1994. The researchers also pointed out that at a time of widespread educational reform it was not possible to attribute changes in the number of offenders in schools entirely to EPOC. The evaluation identified a number of difficulties that affected the initiative, including problems securing co - operation between the youth service and the police. It also noted with concern the lack of involvement of school teaching staff beyond those who were members of the Youth Affairs Group. The authors, nevertheless, concluded that schools were probably better placed than any other agency to co-ordinate multi-agency initiatives among young people. They also argued that Youth Affairs Groups were a model worth replicating to deliver a social education programme with a wider focus, aimed at families as well as individuals (Galloway and Smith, unpublished).

Funding and costs: he project was funded by a DfE grant of £235,000. The evaluation was funded by a Home Office grant of £30,000.

Schools Crime Awareness and Reduction Programme (SCARP)

Brief description: the programme is designed to raise awareness of crime issues among school pupils and make them think carefully about their own behaviour and their rights and duties as citizens. They are involved in problem-solving activities to help them make informed choices when subject to peer pressure that could lead them to break the law. The scheme has been funded by Durham County Council Youth Justice team in response to the Children Act requirement to "encourage children within their area not to commit crimes".

Location: forty junior and secondary schools in County Durham. SCARP has provided consultancy services and materials to schools and local authorities outside the county, by request.

Programmes: SCARP's work in schools is concerned with the cross-curricular themes of citizenship and health education. Programmes are tailored to the requirements of individual schools within a broad framework of six modules:

- law and order

- peer pressure

- substance use and abuse

- courts

- child employment

- divided families.

Quizzes, games, questionnaires, demonstrated role play and other active learning techniques are used to stimulate discussion and participation.

Outcomes: after taking part in a lesson, pupils complete a questionnaire testing their understanding of the issues raised, its relevance to their own lives and their views about the way the session was presented. They are also asked how they felt the session content could help them – either through supportive information or by dissuading them from involvement in potential criminal activities, including drug misuse. Results for 1995–6 suggest that most pupils absorb positive messages.

Funding and costs: SCARP's budget for 1996–7 is £35,000, including a co - ordinator (35 hours per week), assistant co - ordinator (25 hours) and sessional facilitators. Its principal funder is Durham County Council (partly through DfEE GEST funding) . The assistant co - ordinator is funded by Durham Constabulary. Other funding has come through Rural Development Commission and through district councils (including money from the Single Regeneration Budget).

4 Sport and leisure

Introduction

Sports, outdoor pursuits and constructive leisure activities are a well-established feature of initiatives whose aim is to divert juvenile offenders and young people 'at risk' away from crime. Such schemes currently cover a spectrum that includes:

- holiday activities for children

- individual and team sports

- outdoor adventure activities

- recreation and leisure pursuits

- youth work.

Despite a long-held presumption among policy makers and practitioners that sport and other physically demanding activities have a part to play in preventing criminality, the evidence to support their view is limited (Coalter, 1988; Robins, 1990). Researchers face a number of obstacles:

- Not all sports are distinguished by a sense of fair play and an absence of criminal associations, although the personal qualities of successful sports men and women – their sense of achievement, discipline, commitment, channelled aggression and willingness to abide by the rules – are in contrast to those of most offenders and young people at risk.

- Those who take up sports are self-selecting, it is hard to determine whether sport reduces the risks of offending or whether it simply attracts young people who are predisposed to conform (Coalter, 1988; Robins, 1990; Barrett, 1994; Barrett, 1995).

- Anecdotal reports leave no doubt that community-based programmes

55

that include a physically demanding adventure experience have given some young people at risk the opportunity to change the direction of their lives (Hunt, 1989; Barrett, 1995). However, matters as mundane as the weather may influence the quality of the outdoor experience, ensuring that no two programmes are strictly comparable or replicable (Bates, 1993).

- There is a shortage of reliable information regarding which aspects of sport, adventure and leisure pursuit programmes are most effective and for how long. It is not clear which interventions are most appropriate for different groups of young people (Barrett, 1995).

Reviews of the available studies in this area support the view that merely introducing young people at risk of offending to sport or adventure activities is unlikely to reduce criminality (Coalter, 1988). Initiatives need to be part of a wider programme that addresses other aspects of their lives at home, at school and in the community. Their effectiveness is likely to depend on whether they achieve at least some of the following:

- improvements in cognitive and social skills

- reductions in impulsiveness and risk-taking behaviour

- raised self-esteem and self - confidence

- improvements in education and employment prospects.

Some studies of outdoor adventure programmes in America and New Zealand have concluded that they achieved reductions in criminal behaviour in the short term, but could have done better if their effects had been reinforced with follow-up programmes in the community (Winterdyk and Griffiths, 1984; Fyfe, 1990).

Among current preventive work in the UK that contains a sport, outdoor adventure or 'constructive use of leisure' element are initiatives provided by, or in partnership with, the youth justice sections of social services departments and the Probation Service. There is also the work of the statutory youth services (including Youth Action programmes backed by the DfEE's Grants for Educational Support and Training [GEST]) and of youth and community development initiatives provided by sporting organisations and by public and voluntary agencies.

In terms of reducing crime and criminality, project work in this area tends to blur the boundaries and distinctions between different target groups:

- generalised youth projects in disadvantaged communities often find themselves working with a high proportion of young people who have already been cautioned or convicted in a juvenile court

- some probation and youth justice projects are used by young people 'at risk' who are not subject to a court order

- Some youth organisations, as a matter of deliberate practice, provide activities for mixed groups of offenders and non-offenders.

Some researchers have argued that youth work in particular could play a more active and constructive part in diverting young people away from crime (Graham and Smith, 1994). Practitioners have been urged to increase their awareness of risk factors in young people's backgrounds and to provide activities that promote specific social skills as a means of prevention (Huskins, 1996).

The projects described in this chapter are grouped under three headings:

- Constructive use of leisure

  Ilderton Motor Project

  Millwall Community Sports Scheme

  Peterborough L.I.N.C.

  Sports Counselling (Hampshire and West Yorkshire)

  Staffordshire Police Activity and Community Enterprise (SPACE)

- Outdoor Pursuits

  Fairbridge

  Outward Bound Access Programme

  Mobex (Merseyside)

- Youth Work

  Runcorn Youth Action Project

  Welland Youth Action Scheme

  Youth at Risk

Constructive use of leisure

Ilderton Motor Project

Brief description: launched in 1974, Ilderton is the oldest among more than 60 motor projects in England and Wales intended to prevent offending and reoffending among young people – especially the taking of cars without their owners' consent ('TWOCking'). The course content of these projects varies, but the usual aim is to make young people aware of the dangers of illegal, unskilled driving while enabling them to pursue a constructive and legitimate interest in cars (Martin and Webster, 1994).

Location: Deptford, South East London.

Referrals: probation officers and social workers refer young people aged 13 to 25, the majority of whom have been involved in motor crime. Most have been cautioned, but not convicted. Only a minority are serving probation orders (Martin and Webster, 1994). The project accepts around 20 members at any one time.

Programme: the core activity is teaching car mechanics and maintenance by restoring old cars that can be used for 'banger' racing. Participants are organised in teams and not allowed to take part in race meetings unless they attend at least two of the four nightly sessions each week. One of these must be the weekly meeting when progress is discussed and the group can impose sanctions for any anti-social behaviour, in or outside the workshop, that might reflect on the project. The project's cars are raced competitively at off-road tracks around 15 times a year.

Outcomes: a 1994 report for the Home Office found that although less ambitious than some motor projects the Ilderton scheme was 'a well-tried and efficient operation' working with more than 50 young people a year. The target of each member attending eight sessions a month was (probably) being achieved. It was not, however, clear how far the project succeeded in diverting offenders from custody (Martin and Webster, 1994). They expressed the view that preventive work with young people at risk was the core activity of motor projects, rather than the rehabilitation of known offenders. A subsequent evaluation of the Ilderton project by the Inner London Probation Service found that a sample of 30 clients who had been referred were significantly less likely to have reoffended in the following three years than a matched comparison group of 40 clients with similar histories of car crime (62 per cent compared with 100 per cent). They were also less likely to have been sentenced to custody for further offences (15 per cent compared with 46 per cent of the comparison group). There was a decline in the proportion of TWOC offences recorded among the Ilderton group from 75 per cent of all offences to less than half (Wilkinson and Morgan,1995).

Funding and costs: Ilderton Motor Project is administered as a company limited by guarantee with charitable status. Staff salaries are paid directly by the Inner London Probation Service. The 1994 Home Office report on motor projects estimated its annual running costs at more than £70,000 a year. Assuming attendance by 52 members in a full year, it calculated the unit cost per member at £1,350 a year (or £30 a week), (Martin and Webster, 1994). The Inner London Probation Service evaluation combined this figure with estimates by Coopers & Lybrand (Coopers & Lybrand, 1994) of the possible costs of crime and different criminal justice disposals. It arrived at a suggestion that probation use of Ilderton Motor Project might be saving the community between £150,000 and £300,000 a year (Wilkinson and Morgan, 1995). In 1996, the project was awarded a National Lottery grant of £160,000 over two years to extend its education and training work. Deptford Task Force and Deptford City Challenge have contributed 'matched' grants of £22,000 and £20,000 respectively.

Millwall Community Sports Scheme

Brief description: Millwall Football Club is host to one of the longest established 'Football in the Community' initiatives in the country. In addition to programmes that encourage sporting activity in local schools and estates, it is closely involved in education and training schemes for persistent school truants and excluded pupils, young offenders and unemployed young people. A *Sports Scholarship* scheme helps around 15 young people a year to pursue an interest in sport in tandem with academic study.

Location: Millwall FC's ground ('The New Den') in South Bermondsey, London and the surrounding boroughs of Southwark and Lewisham.

Referrals: participants in the truancy project are referred by Lewisham secondary schools. The *Kickstart* project is open to unemployed young people who lack basic qualifications. Referrals to the weekly 'young offender' session are from the Inner London Probation Service. Students for the *Sports Scholarship* scheme are aged 16 to 25 and drawn from the catchment area for Deptford City Challenge.

Programmes: core activities include 22 weekly sport sessions in local schools. The aim is to stimulate children's interest in football and other games while encouraging 'sportsmanlike' behaviour, including playing by the rules, respect for an opponent and learning how to win and lose. The scheme, which is managed by a former Football League professional player, runs weekly coaching and play sessions for children and teenagers on a number of estates.

Truancy project: up to 15 persistent secondary school non-attenders spend one day a week at the club for a combination of educational, sporting and crime prevention activities. Classroom sessions, in one of the club's executive lounges, follow a curriculum which uses football and other subjects of immediate interest to teach basic mathematics, English and other core subjects. Police are invited to talk to the group about crime, its victims and the criminal justice system. Participation in the afternoon sport session is conditional on good behaviour during the morning. As a further reward for regular attendance, participants receive free tickets to Millwall home matches.

Kickstart: the year-long course takes unemployed, poorly qualified school leavers for 16 hours a week, spending time at Lewisham College learning basic writing, communication and computer skills while pursuing their sports interests and working with the Millwall community scheme in schools. Students can gain a Community Sports Leaders Award leading to an NVQ (Level One) in sport and recreation. The course has built a working relationship with the Metropolitan Police College at Hendon where students assist in discussion groups and 'role play' training sessions.

Sports Scholarships: bursaries of up to £1,000 a year allow young people from disadvantaged backgrounds with sporting talent to improve their skills while pursuing a course leading to a vocational or higher education qualification.

Outcomes: there has been no detailed evaluation of outcomes from the Millwall community projects.

- An internal review of the first year of **Kickstart** concluded that students had mostly taken full advantage of the sport leader courses on offer and achieved a good range of qualifications (Jones, 1995). This convinced the main funders that it would be worth extending the scheme. In 1994-5, 60 per cent of students gained an NVQ Level One and 80 per cent went on to further education.

- Monitoring of the truancy project for 1994-5 found that at least 10 out of 15 pupils (all boys) returned to school full-time at the start of 1995-6.

- Out of 16 Sports Scholars in 1994-5, three found immediate full-time employment, six were working on a casual or voluntary basis and the remainder continued in full-time education, including one young woman embarking on an education degree course in Canterbury. The scholars included an international male sprinter and two members of the England women's soccer team.

Funding and costs: Millwall Community Sports Scheme receives core annual grants in excess of £50,000 from the London Boroughs of Lewisham and Southwark, Millwall FC and the Professional Footballers Association. The estates project is funded by the Single Regeneration Budget and Deptford City Challenge. The latter also provided £20,000 during 1995–6 towards the Sports Scholarship scheme.

S.P.A.C.E. ('Staffordshire Police Activity and Community Enterprise')

Brief description: police-organised summer play schemes for children and young people have been running for 14 years in Staffordshire. The county-wide programme remains one of the most carefully monitored projects among the many SPLASH! ('Schools and Police Liaison Activities for the Summer Holidays') and other holiday schemes that have followed its example in many other parts of the country.[1]

Location: four weeks in August at 23 locations in Staffordshire.

Referrals: young people aged 10 to 16 can register.

Programmes: schemes are organised locally in all ten county police divisions with varying programmes of play activities and trips. All schemes include a 'drop-in' centre that is open every day so that young people who cannot afford the extra costs of outings can still take part in enjoyable activities. In addition, there are centrally organised 'camps' held each day at Staffordshire Police's outward bound centre as well as community safety training days, a five-a-side football competition, a multi-ethnic 'international day' and a concluding carnival held at the Staffordshire County Showground.

Outcomes: a 1986 Home Office evaluation of S.P.A.C.E. found that 25 per cent of 10- to- 14- year-olds in Staffordshire had registered for the scheme, rising to 30 per cent in some high crime, urban areas. A random sample suggested that between 7.5 per cent and 17 per cent of participants in individual schemes were 'known to the police' – mostly as a result of being cautioned. The researchers were wary about attributing comparatively low August figures for burglary and other property crimes in Staffordshire during the mid-1980s to introduction of the county-wide scheme (Heal and Laycock, 1987). They concluded that the changes in crime patterns "probably came about for a number of reasons, possibly including the impact of the holiday scheme". An internal police review has since argued that the value of S.P.A.C.E. lies in its ability to increase the type and number of non-criminal opportunities available to young people rather than the 'inconclusive' evidence regarding crime levels during August (Staffordshire Police, 1994). In 1990, S.P.A.C.E. attracted 23,600 registrations, which had declined by 1993 to 15,200. This reflected the growing strength in some

---

1. See, for example, Crime Concern (1994) SPLASH. *Summer Holiday Activities for young people.* A guide for scheme organisers.

areas of local authority playschemes catering for a wider age range, as well as a doubling of the S.P.A.C.E. registration fee from £1 to £2. This and the heavy commitment of police time required to run the scheme led to a decision to seek local authority support in converting S.P.A.C.E. into a multi-agency project (Staffordshire Police, 1994).

Funding and costs: the S.P.A.C.E. budget for 1992 was £338,000, financed by local fund-raising activities, donations from charitable trusts, businesses and local authorities. It was estimated that the costs would have been well over £500,000 if police manpower costs had been included. In addition to 112 operational police officers, the scheme involved over 800 unpaid civilian helpers and 89 unpaid volunteer staff from the Probation Service and other agencies.

Peterborough City L.I.N.C. (Littlehey Incentive for New Careers)

Brief description: this summer activity scheme for teenagers 'at risk' of offending is believed to be unique in its use of facilities, staff and support from inmates at a Category 'C' closed prison.

Location: Peterborough and H.M.P. Littlehey, Cambridgeshire.

Referrals: young men and women aged 15 to 17 from socially disadvantaged neighbourhoods are referred by police, probation, teachers, social services, the youth service and parents. Participants, who are selected by an interview panel, must agree to 'give something back' to the community such as fund raising for the following year's project.

Programme: the four - week summer programme runs for seven hours a day, five days a week, for three weeks, plus a one week 'residential' of outdoor activities. Prison Service physical education instructors and inmates help run the course inside Littlehey which gives participants the opportunity to achieve a Community Sports Leaders Award (CSLA), First Aid Certificates and other basic qualifications. The venue and contact with prison inmates is designed to encourage discussion about crime and imprisonment and to "allow young people to explore the realities of the possible consequences of their own actions" (Cambridgeshire County Council, 1995).

Outcomes: monitoring for 1994 shows that the scheme was attended by nine young people of whom five gained the CSLA qualification. The one week residential included sailing, canoeing and windsurfing at the UK Sailing Academy on the Isle of Wight. There has been no evaluation of offending behaviour, but there are anecdotal accounts of participants being positively influenced by their encounters with prison and prisoners. Schools have reported positively on changed attitudes among pupils who have been referred.

Funding and costs: the cost of the 1994 project was estimated at between £300 and £350 per participant. The figure would have been substantially higher if the Prison Service had made any charge for staff time and use of its facilities. The project's other sponsors were Cambridgeshire County Council, Peterborough City Council, The Prince's Trust, Pearl Assurance and Exel Logistics. A number of bursaries were made available by the UK Sailing Academy.

Sports counselling (Hampshire and West Yorkshire)

Brief description: 'Sports counselling' is a term that describes projects whose aim is to reduce crime and criminality by encouraging young people to make constructive use of their leisure time. It is an approach that has been applied in two locations with clients of probation and youth justice. Most of those taking part have had criminal convictions.

- The Sports Counselling Scheme in Hampshire grew from an initiative suggested by a Southampton magistrate in the early 1980s and began as part of the Manpower Services Commission's Community Programme. It became part of Hampshire Probation Service and, from 1986 to 1989, was among a number of 'participation demonstration projects' supported by the Sports Council.

- West Yorkshire Sports Counselling Project was started by a former staff member of the Hampshire scheme and worked with probation and youth justice referrals between March 1993 and March 1996. It was Home Office funded and - unlike the Hampshire scheme - was established as a voluntary organisation working in 'partnership' with youth justice and probation. At the end of 1995, West Yorkshire Probation Service sought tenders for the future management of the project based on a reduction in length of the basic programme from 12 sessions to four (extendible to eight). West Yorkshire Sports Counselling argued that the new conditions would undermine the quality of their work and were not awarded the contract. An evaluation by Sheffield University researchers was published in March 1996. Although acknowledging some difficulties inherent in reconviction rate studies, they found a significant reduction in re-offending among probation clients who had participated for between eight and 12 weeks, but not for a shorter involvement (Nichols and Taylor, 1996).

Location: the Hampshire scheme has its main office in Southampton and employs 'activity officers' on the Isle of Wight and in the towns of Portsmouth, Basingstoke and Aldershot. The West Yorkshire Sports Counselling Association was based in Castleford and maintained a full-time sports leader in Leeds and part-time counselling staff in the boroughs of Bradford, Calderdale, Kirklees and Wakefield. The new contractor, Yorkshire Adventure Sports, is based in Harrogate.

Referrals: individuals in Hampshire and West Yorkshire are referred by probation or youth justice case workers after being interviewed about their spare time and interests. Most of the 550 referrals in Hampshire each year are aged between 16 and 24. In 1991 the basic programme was reduced from 12 to eight sessions and, in 1995, to four (see below).

Programme: both projects aim to reduce the rate of reoffending. Trained staff are used to:

• help, befriend and advise participants on a one-to-one basis while pursuing constructive activities

• help participants to obtain concessionary passes for using local sport and leisure centres

• create opportunities for participants to pursue outdoor physical activities, including work as conservation volunteers

• encourage continued, independent involvement in activities including club membership, volunteering and training opportunities and achieving sport and leisure qualifications.

Their rationale suggests that individuals who actively pursue a hobby, outdoor activity or sport will not only have less time on their hands to commit crime, but may also gain in self-esteem, self-confidence and social skills – drawing them towards training, employment and a less anti-social lifestyle. The fact that individuals take part voluntarily is considered essential to this process (Nichols and Taylor, 1994).

Hampshire – participants are invited to choose from a menu of sport and leisure pursuits ranging from weight training, squash, martial arts and swimming to fishing, bird watching and metal detecting. They complete a health and fitness questionnaire (including advice on the harmful effects of smoking, drinking and drugs) and are helped to apply for a concessionary pass to their local leisure centre. Efforts are made to ensure that the first session occurs as soon as possible after the interview – ideally that afternoon or the next day. Even so, this is the point at which a significant proportion of referrals are lost (see below).The emphasis is on informal, non-competitive participation. It is thought that setting a premium on sporting skill or achievement would compound the low sense of self-worth that characterises many young offenders. One-to-one sessions are taken as an opportunity to find out more about the participant's background and interests. After four sessions, participants may be referred to a volunteer prepared to help them pursue their chosen activity further. Others may be introduced to a local sports club - although the costs of membership and travel, as well as the expected levels of skill and commitment, create difficulties. The project organises group outings for canoeing and other outdoor pursuits, and has referred individuals to adventure training courses and conservation programmes, such as the volunteers scheme run by the Prince's Trust. Other referrals have been to further education, training and employment services.[2]

West Yorkshire - although in many respects similar to the Hampshire model, the West Yorkshire Sports Counselling Association provided a maximum 12-week programme of three-hour sessions. A working relationship was established with local authorities and sports leaders were based in the offices of local authority sports development sections. The project had good access to municipal sports centres and programmes showed a discernible bias towards sport, as distinct from leisure activities. Outdoor pursuits were available as part of the basic programme.

Outcomes: Hampshire–in addition to annual monitoring, the Hampshire scheme (then known as the Solent Sports Counselling Project) was evaluated by the Sports Council Research Unit between April 1987 and 1989. This included an examination of police records for a small random sample of 42 participants. The present scheme, offering four weekly sessions, is different to that operating in the late 1980s which was, itself, modified during the evaluation period to introduce a 12-session structure. The individuals in the random sample had all participated before March 1988, when the counselling commitment was more open-ended. The main findings were that:

• those taking part had convictions ranging between vandalism and malicious wounding, but most had been involved in crimes against property

• almost half had four or more convictions

• all but two of the 13 clients who participated for less than three weeks were charged with further offences in the following 12 months

• there were 18 participants who faced no further charges in the following year. These included 14 who had been intensively involved with the project and four who had attended for four or five weeks

• another six participants who faced further charges after leaving the programme appeared to have reduced their rate of offending (Sports Council Research Unit (North West), 1989).

---

2. Hampshire Probation Service, at the time of writing, was bringing the Sports Couselling scheme and Community Link Team together under the same management, to create a 'one stop shop' for promoting education training, employment and leisure opportunities among offenders.

Drawing on these statistics and positive case histories the researchers concluded that the project had enjoyed significant success in helping to halt long-term recidivism among participants, including some with histories of serious crime. They also reported the view of probation officers that the project was instrumental in some cases in allowing young offenders to break away from a criminal sub-culture[3] Monitoring of the 12-session programme indicated a substantial early drop-out rate among referrals that has remained a feature of the scheme. Annual figures for an eight-session programme, run between 1991 and mid-1995 showed that between 13 and 24 per cent of referrals failed to attend the first interview. Only half those who start the programme attended more than four sessions – one of the factors that prompted a further reduction in the basic programme.

West Yorkshire – an evaluation by the University of Sheffield's Leisure Management Unit between March 1993 and December 1995 found comparable attrition in numbers (Nichols and Taylor, 1994 and 1996). Out of 329 referrals, 212 did not complete the programme, including 131 who never started. One reason for the early drop-out rate was a waiting list which reflected a high level of demand and the popularity of the programme among probation/youth justice workers. Although 113 participants completed the 12-session programme, the numbers each year (46 in 1994 and 40 in 1995) fell short of the performance target of 60 set by the Home Office. The Sheffield researchers compared two-year reconviction rates among 38 participants with those for a matched group of probation clients who had not attended sports counselling. There was no significant differences for those who had spent seven weeks or less on the programme, but those who had attended for between eight and 12 weeks were significantly less likely to have been convicted for further offences. A separate analysis used a formula devised for the Home Office to compare a reconviction rate of 49 per cent for those who completed eight to 12 weeks of sports counselling with a prediction score based on age and offending record of 64 per cent.[4] Questionnaires identified improvements in participants' self-esteem and perceptions of their own fitness. There was evidence that the sports leaders had been accepted as friends and role models.

Funding and costs: sports counselling in Hampshire has a devolved Probation Service budget for 1996/7 of £163,000. The cost of the West Yorkshire Sports Counselling Project in 1995/6 was £108,000 including £70,000 on salaries and £9,700 for evaluation research. This was mostly covered by a Home Office (Supervision Grants to Voluntary Organisations) contribution to West Yorkshire Probation Service.

Comment: like other projects described in this chapter, there is no suggestion that sport or leisure activities in themselves have the power to

---

3.   Robins, D. (1990) highlights the difficulty of knowing from the Hampshire evaluation what, if any, changes in offending behaviour were causally linked to participation in sports counselling.

4.   One difficulty identified by the researchers is the possibility that participants who completed the course were by definition more stable and better motivated than others, making them less likely to commit further offences. However, the use of case histories, interviews and questionnaires supported a view that at least part of the lower reconviction rate was attributable to sustained involvement in the course.

reduce criminality.

- The constructive use of leisure time, improved self-esteem and a positive relationship with the sports counsellor appear more influential than the choice of activity. So, too, are opportunities that may arise to find training and work or to associate with new, non-delinquent friends.

- The West Yorkshire evaluation was focused on young offenders, rather than young people at risk of offending. But its findings include a number of general messages about the effective use of constructive leisure opportunities in criminality prevention. Among the factors contributing to success, it identifies :

  - voluntary participation

  - one-to-one counselling

  - the skills of staff serving as 'brokers of opportunities'

  - staff commitment (including unofficial follow-up work with clients who had completed the programme).

- The high proportion of referrals failing to complete (or even begin) the programme influenced the decision by West Yorkshire Probation Service to reduce the length of sports counselling to a basic four-sessions with a contract specifying a minimum 100 completions a year. However, the subsequently-published Sheffield evaluation concluded that a minimum eight weeks was needed to be effective in reducing reoffending.

Outdoor pursuits

Fairbridge
Outward Bound Access Programmes

Brief description: Fairbridge and the Outward Bound Trust are two experienced providers of personal development programmes in which demanding outdoor activities play a prominent part. Both charities have worked extensively with young offenders and young people 'at risk' of offending. Similarities of approach mean that their projects are described here under a single heading. Both emphasise the importance of working with young people in their own communities before and after their adventure experience. Fairbridge–through an associate charity, The Venture Trust – is the chosen provider for the three-year experimental Applecross Project which the Home Office is funding for young offenders, aged 16 to 25 (Home Office, 1995a and b), (see below). Following its merger with the

Duke of Edinburgh Award scheme, the Outward Bound Trust discontinued the Access Programmes. Consultations were taking place at the time of writing as to how the work should be taken forward.

Location: Fairbridge is based in 10 cities around the UK. It runs a residential training centre at Applecross on the North West coast of Scotland and owns a 'tall' ship, The Spirit of Scotland, based on the River Clyde. The Outward Bound Access Programmes operated in Belfast, Coventry, Merseyside and Tyneside making use of the trust's outdoor training centres in a number of different locations.

Referrals: Fairbridge caters for young people aged 14 to 25 who are unemployed and deemed at risk of social alienation, including truancy, exclusion from school, long-term unemployment, drug misuse and crime. Referrals come from social services, educational welfare officers and through partnership contracts with probation. Fairbridge also uses outreach work and 'drop-in' facilities in the cities where it is based, to make contact with young people who might benefit (Fairbridge, 1995). The Outward Bound Access Programmes were designed for disaffected young people aged 13 to 19 from disadvantaged neighbourhoods. Most were found to have been involved in criminal activities.[5]

Programmes: Fairbridge states that its programme: "encourages active learning to both raise awareness of, and challenge, attitudes, values and behaviour".

The programme is delivered in three phases:

- *Induction:* two days are spent explaining the programme and seeking a voluntary commitment from young people to participate in the basic course and beyond. 'Ice-breaker' sessions are included, giving an introduction to outdoor activities. Individuals are asked to contribute £15 towards the cost.

- *The Basic Course:* takes place over seven or eight days. It begins at a Fairbridge team centre with the participants working in groups of eight to 12. Each group includes, so far as possible, a mix of males and females, ethnic backgrounds and offenders and non-offenders. Planning sessions and group work exercises are used to encourage co-operation and trust. Local sport and leisure facilities are visited to learn basic skills in preparation for the planned outdoor pursuit(s). The group transfers to a residential outdoor activities centre where they learn to work and live together as a team, while taking part in physically challenging activities such as climbing, canoeing, abseiling, ropes courses, hill walking and orienteering. The programme usually includes an overnight expedition.

---

5. The Access Programme also included courses for young people with disabilities.

- *Follow through:* takes place in the community and is designed so each participant can prepare and implement a personal action plan. Criminal and other anti-social behaviour is confronted as individuals review their past life and future aims. The support offered includes personal development groups and workshops and help finding further education, training or job placements. Participants have the opportunity to become involved in constructive leisure activities, including work on community and environmental projects. Further expeditions may be arranged and the sailing ship, *The Spirit of Scotland,* is used for individuals who may benefit from an additional challenge (This can include those who fail to contribute their group as well as those who show an aptitude for outdoor pursuits).

The Applecross Project: The experimental programme, fully-funded by the Home Office (Home Office 1995b)., was scheduled to run for three years from November 1995. The individuals taking part are volunteers, but it differs from the model described above in a number of important respects:

- two thirds of referrals are convicted offenders, subject to probation orders; the remaining third are 'youth at risk' referred by other agencies

- the residential courses, which take place at the Applecross Centre, last for 21 days – three times the length of a Fairbridge basic course. The curriculum allows for two challenging 'wilderness' expeditions, community service projects, first aid instruction and training in personal and social skills

- follow through in the community remains an important part of the overall package, but work on a personal action plan will begin at an early stage during the course.

Outward Bound Access Programmes – In the early 1980s, the Outward Bound Trust placed youth workers in a number of cities to make contact with local youth agencies who might use its outdoor courses, including those working with young people at risk of offending. The initiative was criticised for lack of focus and a 1991 HMI Report found that the residential centre courses were poorly attuned to the needs of disadvantaged youth (Dept. for Education and Science, 1991). The Access Programmes were a response to those concerns and their implications for staff training. The main components were:

- Taster days: which allowed a group of young people referred by a particular agency to find out more about Outward Bound and participate in two or three outdoor activities. Agencies were expected to nominate a 'key worker' for each group who would take part in subsequent sessions, especially the residential course.

- Community programme: this took place over six days during which participants acquired basic skills for their outward bound course. Groups, typically with 10 to 12 members, were expected to choose and plan the activities they would pursue, setting their own objectives. Those that showed no sign of working as a team risked being disbanded. Groups were expected to organise fund-raising towards the cost (25%) of their residential course.

- Outward Bound Course: a minimum eight days was recommended for the residential course, although 12 days was considered optimum. Outdoor activities varied according to the plans devised by individual groups (some opted for wilderness expeditions lasting the entire week). Individuals were helped to prepare action plans for when they returned home, but the group was also expected to plan its future activities collectively.

- Follow through work: groups continued to meet for discussion and leisure activities while individuals were offered help in implementing their plans. There was a phased withdrawal of staff support, usually over six months.

Unlike Fairbridge, the Outward Bound Access Programmes did not seek to achieve groups with a mix of backgrounds. Members of a group were usually referred by the same agency, came from the same geographical area and often already knew each other. This enabled group work to begin in the community before the residential course and to continue there afterwards. Some groups continued to meet and provide mutual support after the programme had been completed.

Outcomes: neither programme has been subjected to rigorous, external evaluation. However, both have produced monitoring results that suggest some success in reducing criminality among a range of positive outcomes.

- National statistics for Fairbridge course participants (including non-offenders) suggest that 10 per cent find jobs by the end of the programme, 30 per cent go on to further education, 20 per cent join training schemes and 25 per cent take part in voluntary community projects (Fairbridge, 1995).

- Monitoring of a two - year partnership between Fairbridge and Northumbria Probation Service, funded by the Home Office, found 81 per cent of participants did not reoffend within a year, eight per cent found jobs, 10 per cent joined training schemes and two per cent took up further education (Fairbridge, 1995).

- Early results from research by Kent Probation Service suggested a 48 per cent reoffending rate over three years for clients who complete a

Fairbridge course. These are reported to be recidivist offenders for whom the Home Office prediction score would be an 85 per cent reoffending rate (Whitfield, 1995).

- Monitoring of the Outward Bound Access Programmes on Merseyside suggested that 80 per cent of 'at risk' participants had not engaged in criminal activity within six months of completing the residential course (Outward Bound Access Programmes).

- 'Positive' outcomes were reported for 70 per cent of participants, ranging from training and further education to volunteer work and assisting in other Outward Bound projects.

Funding and costs: Fairbridge – works in partnership with Probation and Youth Justice services, charging a (negotiable) fee for its services. It also receives funding from the Home Office, government urban regeneration programmes, local government, charitable trusts and sponsors in the private sector. Individual participants are asked for a small contribution towards the costs of their course (see above).

The average cost of a local Fairbridge team is estimated at £160,000 a year including salaries for seven members of staff. Course unit costs are estimated at £63 per participant/day, suggesting a total cost for a typical 17-day course of £1,071 per trainee. (If the organisation's regional and national costs were included, the cost per participant/day would be closer to £100.)

Outward Bound Access Programmes were supported by a three year grant of £50,000 a year tapering to £40,000 in the third year from the DfEE. Half the cost of the residential course (£50 per person per night) was met by the Outward Bound Trust with the remainder coming from the referral agency and the participants themselves. Fund - raising was considered a helpful part of the learning process, but no participant was barred because they could not pay their share. A residential course of 12 nights for a group of 10 cost around £6,000. The cost of the taster days, community programme and follow-through was around £1,500, excluding overheads.

Comment: both programmes include a clear rationale and method for working with youth at risk and young offenders:

- they target disaffected young people from disadvantaged communities, although not those who exhibit an extreme level of psychosocial disorder and anti-social behaviour

- demanding physical activities are used to motivate young people, improve their self-confidence and teach them social skills, including teamwork and a sense of responsibility towards others. They are treated as a means, not an end in themselves

- the 'follow through' phase after the outdoor residential is a key feature, allowing participants to receive practical advice and help in implementing a personal action plan

- participation in these programmes is voluntary–an aspect that the organisers insist is fundamental to achieving young people's co-operation

- because those taking part are self-selecting, they may not be altogether typical of young people at risk of offending. Monitoring results suggest that the majority of those who take part are able to make at least some changes in their lives

- in the case of known offenders, there are indications from the monitoring data that programmes of this kind can achieve reductions in reoffending.

Mobex (Merseyside)

Brief description: Mobex (Mobile Expedition Unit) Merseyside was the first of four inner city initiatives set up by the Young Explorers Trust. Now under the aegis of Merseyside Youth Association, the project helps young people to plan and implement their own outdoor ventures and expeditions.

Location: Liverpool.

Referrals: Mobex contacts young people aged 14 to 25 through informal outreach work and referrals from local agencies, including schools, youth clubs, drug prevention groups and social services.

Programme: there is no fixed programme. Groups are presented with a broad range of ideas as to the type of outdoor activities they might wish to pursue. Individuals can choose to join the Duke of Edinburgh Award Scheme or pursue other outdoor and community work qualifications. Groups plan their expeditions in the knowledge that they must raise the money to pay for everything except the project staff. They receive advice on obtaining individual sponsorship and help in drafting applications to charitable trusts. Staff also arrange any training, technical advice, equipment and transport that is needed. The aim is for participants to become as independent and self-sufficient as possible. A feature of the project is its purpose-converted Mercedes van which serves as a mobile meeting room during the planning stage and can subsequently be used for outdoor training and the final expedition. Recent activities have included a winter skills expedition and summer climbing and orienteering in Snowdonia, snow-holing in the

Cairngorms and a Basic Expedition Training Award (BETA) expedition in Yorkshire. A BETA course was arranged during 1996 for members of black and ethnic minority communities. An aid expedition to Romania was organised by young unemployed people and recovering drug users.

Outcomes: there has been no systematic assessment of Mobex, although internal evaluation procedures were being reviewed at the time of writing. The organisers cite anecdotal evidence of individuals whose involvement has helped them to stop offending or misusing drugs and to obtain outdoor or community work qualifications. One former probation client who gained a BETA award through Mobex became a full-time worker for the Outward Bound Trust (Hooper, 1992). Others have gone on to further and higher education, training, volunteering and employment in youth and social work.

Funding and costs: the annual running costs of Mobex is around £40,000. It has been unable to secure sufficient funds in recent years to avoid annual losses. The project manager's salary is currently funded by the Langkelly Foundation.

Youth Work

Runcorn Youth Action Project

Brief description: a detached youth worker was employed between May 1993 and March 1996 as part of an overall crime reduction strategy to make contact with disaffected young people on a socially disadvantaged estate. This allowed the young people themselves to become involved in devising a range of constructive activities aimed at diversion from crime and anti-social behaviour.

Location: the high-crime Castlefields estate on the outskirts of Runcorn and the Halton Village area.

Referrals: the target group for detached youth work were young people at risk of criminal involvement, including rowdy groups of youths who were considered a major problem on the estate.

Programmes: contact between the youth worker and young people led to separate health and activity groups being established for young men and women. The former (with an average attendance of nine) included workshops on sex education, contraception and substance abuse as well as discussion meetings with a community police officer. The 'Girls Let Loose' group covered a wide range of topics including art, presentation skills and a skiing trip as well as personal safety, smoking and drugs. Members carried out a safety survey on the estate which persuaded Halton Borough Council to invest in additional street lighting and to cut back bushes and trees. Other activities arranged as part of the project included a series of well-attended dance workshops, an arts week, a weekly after-school club for younger pupils at a local secondary school and a 'Christmas Rave' organised by a planning group of young people at the estate's community centre. In Halton Village, a disruptive gang of boys who had brought the local youth club to the point of closure were diverted into constructive leisure activities, including conservation work.

Outcomes: an evaluation commissioned by Crime Concern and Cheshire County Council concluded that the use of an experienced youth worker had succeeded in engaging many young people who were outside the reach of existing provision. The scheme gained positive publicity in the local press and 'Girls Let Loose' won a £1,000 prize in the Prudential Youth Action Awards. Although there was no fall in recorded crime on the Castlefield Estate during the first year of the project, there was a 57 per cent decrease in complaints to police about rowdy behaviour by youths. Police, other agencies and members of the local community felt the project had helped build positive relationships with young people where antagonism had previously existed (Webb, 1994).

Funding and costs: the project received £28,000 core funding from Cheshire County Council Youth Service. (It was not supported by the DfEE's GEST programme.)

Welland Youth Action Scheme

Brief description: the Welland Youth Action Scheme is one of 60 youth work projects in 28 local authority areas that have been funded by the Department for Education and Employment's Grants for Education Support and Training (GEST). Like the other programmes, its primary aim has been to produce stimulating and challenging activities for young people at risk of drifting into crime.

Location: the Welland estate on the outskirts of Peterborough.

Referrals: community education, police, probation, social services and schools referred young people aged 13 to 15 known to have committed crime or to have criminal friends or who were in serious difficulty in school (including exclusion).

Programme: a group of 11 young people attended a programme that combined sessions on personal skills and responsibility with a four-week summer holiday project to make a video about young people and life on the estate. They went on to mix sessions concerned with social behaviour with outdoor activities, including a week-long 'residential' at the UK Sailing Academy on the Isle of Wight.

Outcomes: from 17 referrals, the group was rapidly reduced to 11 regular attenders. First year monitoring concluded that the scheme had allowed the young people to receive help with reading and writing, to obtain basic qualifications and begin working as a team. One member of the group was known to have (re)offended (Cambridgeshire County Council, 1994). At the time of writing a national evaluation of the GEST Youth Action Schemes was being completed at Sheffield University. A DfEE circular based on its provisional conclusions is referred to in the final chapter of this report. An earlier survey of Youth Action projects by OFSTED concluded that they displayed much of the richness and variety of good youth work. It found anecdotal evidence that young people at risk had benefited from participation, but called for more effort to involve young women as well as young men (Office for Standards in Education, 1995).

Funding and costs: GEST money for the Youth Action Scheme totalled £3.9 million in 1993–4 and £2.9 million in both 1994–5 and 1995–6.

Youth at Risk UK

Brief description: Youth at Risk works with local authorities and probation to provide a 12 - month programme for young people who exhibit poor emotional adjustment and serious anti-social behaviour. It makes use, in clearly defined roles, of professionals and trained volunteers serving as mentors. Adapted from the 'tough love' movement in the United States, one striking feature of the programme is its use of 'confrontational therapy' during a week-long residential course. The techniques used to persuade young people to recognise the unsatisfactory nature of their current lives and come to terms with painful past experiences became the subject of controversy following a Channel 4 documentary in 1994 (Diverse Productions, 1994). Youth at Risk programmes conducted since 1991 have been monitored and – pending results from a more rigorous evaluation – show some promise in reducing offending and increasing participation in education, training and employment.

Location: the administration is based in Berkshire. Youth at Risk has run two courses for the London Borough of Enfield and three in Sutton. Courses in Portsmouth and Knowsley (Merseyside) were completed in 1996. Courses in Southampton, Nottinghamshire and a second course in Knowsley were in progress at the time of writing.[6]

---

6. Youth at Risk has also provided training for professionals working with young people, including young offenders, in Knowlesley and Northern Ireland.

Referrals: young people aged 14 to 19 are referred by schools, social services, probation and other agencies. Those taking part commonly include a high proportion of young people who have been in local authority care and of recidivist offenders. In terms of criminality prevention, they are drawn from the far end of the spectrum of troubled and troublesome youth (Huskins, 1995).

Programme: the organisers state their aim as creating "a supportive community of professionals, volunteers and young people at risk" in which "all the participants take responsibility for their lives" (Youth at Risk 1994). The programme, offered in partnership with a host agency, consists of:

Enrolment

Young people referred by social services, probation and other agencies attend orientation sessions when the programme is explained in detail. An application form invites them to specify three personal goals they would like to achieve through taking part. Small group sessions underline the need for long-term commitment. Experience suggests that between 80 and 100 referrals may be needed to produce between 25 and 35 participants. The organisers seek to enrol and train between 70 and 120 volunteers from the local community, including those prepared to mentor participants on a one-to-one basis as 'committed partners' (Youth at Risk, 1994).

Residential

The intensive, week-long residential course takes place at Brathay Hall in Cumbria. Volunteers and staff from the host agency are expected to attend and create 'an atmosphere where the young people feel safe to talk about difficult, personal issues. Demanding outdoor activities are used to reinforce a sense of team work and trust. The core sessions are small group and plenary workshops lasting up to five hours. These are led by trained leaders supported by qualified psychotherapists and agency staff. The atmosphere is intense and may lead to disclosures by young people of abuse and other traumatic circumstances. A manager from the local authority is designated to monitor sessions and ensure that child protection policies and procedures are observed. The time is used to confront young people with their anti-social behaviour, to help them confront past experiences and to offer them insight into their own ability to change. At the end of the residential they are introduced to the volunteer mentor who will work with them.

Follow - through

The nine months of follow-through is considered crucial. Weekly group sessions are scheduled during which the young people focus on themselves, their immediate relationships and their communities. 'Cornerstone' themes of recognising new possibilities, taking personal responsibility, demonstrating commitment and supporting other people are examined in detail. Specific topics such as anger management, problem solving, drug abuse, sexual health, further education and careers guidance are covered. Groups are helped to plan their own projects, including community service work and leisure trips and other social activities. Individuals, meanwhile, work towards their personal goals, including qualifications, training and jobs. They are supported by their committed partners through at least one face-to-face meeting and two phone calls per week.

Outcomes: *Participants* - monitoring of the first two courses suggests a high level of initial interest among young people attending orientation sessions, but a subsequent attrition rate of over a third before the residential course. A few participants on both courses (6 and 2) were asked to leave during the week.[7] Young men outnumbered women by more than two to one. Those of either sex who progressed to the follow-through stage included majorities who had:

– been arrested;

– admitted to current drug use;

– had been in care at some time;

– admitted to problems controlling their tempers;

– had experienced violence in their own families;

– lived apart from their natural parents.

Around half had been excluded from school at some time, while small but significant minorities said they had been sexually abused and/or taken a drugs overdose. Multiple arrests related to offences that included armed robbery, street mugging, grievous assault, burglary, taking a vehicle without the owners consent and shoplifting.

Attendance: Half the participants on the first three courses played a full part in the nine month follow through and remained in regular contact with their committed partners. Another one in five attended irregularly.

---

7.   Two 'drop outs' from the first Enfield course subsequently took part in the follow through workshops.

Offending: Youth at Risk's monitoring points to reductions in the numbers involved in drugs and crime and in the frequency of offending for the duration of the course. In Sutton, police records for participants in the year before the course suggest a combined average of 8.75 cautions or convictions per month, which fell to 5.33 in the nine months during the programme–a 40 per cent reduction.[8]

Education: Among nine young people below the school leaving age on the first Sutton course, two pupils improved their attendance and punctuality during the programme and one previous non-attender returned to school. Of four such participants from Enfield, two non - attenders returned to school and one already in school become a regular attender. Five older participants began training for further education.

Employment: Eleven previously unemployed young people obtained jobs during the Sutton course and six remained employed throughout the programme. Ten Enfield participants who had been unemployed had jobs by the end of the programme, while another three had found but then left work during the course.

Volunteering: A third of participants in the courses for which monitoring is available offered their services as volunteers on future programmes.

Funding and costs: the cost of one Youth at Risk programme, including a share of central overheads is put at £184,600 or £229,800 if evaluation and other research costs are included. If 25 young people take part in the residential week and follow-through course, this suggests a cost of more than £9,000 per head (Youth at Risk, 1995). In addition, host and other agencies must take into account their own staff costs and overheads in designing and delivering the course. Although Youth at Risk is now working with other local authorities, the London Borough of Enfield has decided against further involvement because of financial constraints. The first Enfield/NACRO course was funded entirely by voluntary contributions and Youth at Risk continues to depend on grants from charitable trusts, Training and Enterprise Councils and private sector donors. The Sutton courses have received money from the Single Regeneration Budget (SRB) and those in Knowsley have been supported by the European Social Fund. Fees from local authorities during 1995 were budgeted to cover less than half of anticipated revenue. Youth at Risk has the declared objective of eventually obtaining all or most of the basic cost of programmes from the private sector, local authorities and other government sources.

Comment: the promise of Youth at Risk lies in its capacity to achieve results with young people whose problems, including anti-social and criminal behaviour, are especially intractable. They are young people who lack self

---

8.   The organisers point out that this unit calculation takes no account of the benefit to volunteers, local agencies and communities as a whole from the programme and associated training.

confidence and motivation, who are often without stable family backgrounds and whose poor performance in school has left them with few expectations. They are, however, 'self-selecting' in the sense that they represent only a third of those originally referred and agree to take part after strenuous efforts to inform them of the likely demands.

• Independent evaluation would help to establish whether Youth at Risk is effective in the longer-term. Dependable evidence of success is especially desirable given the relatively high cost of the programme and the controversy surrounding some of its methods.

• John Huskins–a former Schools HMI with a specialist interest in youth work – has distributed an assessment paper, 1995, which reports favourably on his impressions of the residential course and follow through. He recommends that Youth at Risk should:

    – provide a clearer description of the rationale for using confrontation therapy and other methods;

    – take steps to gain the co-operation of a wider range of agencies, including education and youth work;

    – define its role by ensuring that it really does target the most damaged and difficult young people with whom most other agencies have failed.

• Therapeutic work with socially and emotionally damaged young people demands a high level of professional skill and experience. Youth at Risk UK, having used American practitioners for its initial courses, will need to demonstrate that the necessary expertise continues to be available.

5 Conclusion

Criminological research spread over half a century has demonstrated with considerable consistency that there are influences in the backgrounds of children and young people that make it more – or less – likely that they will behave anti-socially and commit crime. The question this report has addressed is whether that fund of academic knowledge has a practical application through programmes that prevent crime by reducing criminality.

Research has identified a range of risk factors. These cannot individually be said to 'cause' delinquency, but they help to identify the most promising areas for practical prevention initiatives. Their value as targeting tools is increased by the outcomes of a number of well-designed and evaluated interventions – mostly American – that endorse the view that criminality reduction programmes have a serious and cost-effective part to play in preventing crime (Farrington, 1996).

Promising approaches

No evaluations of programmes in the United Kingdom have, to date, included a long-term commitment to discovering whether a preventive initiative during children's early years can lead to a reduced level of delinquency a decade later. Indeed, many of the family support and education projects described in this report do not list the prevention of delinquency among their stated aims.

Even so, it is appropriate to describe certain projects as 'promising'. This report has presented a sample of British programmes that address important risk factors associated with criminality – the 'intervening variables' – even though the long-term outcomes in terms of offending are unknown. The educational benefits of children receiving some form of quality pre-school education are, for example, well-established (Sylva, 1994). Likewise, anti-bullying initiatives in primary schools have been shown to reduce levels of anti-social behaviour (Smith and Sharp, 1994).

The case for investment in criminality reduction in the UK would be strengthened if future development work in this area were subject to independent, rigorous evaluation. A great deal is known about the correlates of offending, but there is still much to be learned about what constitute the most effective methods of intervention.

It is difficult to make large claims regarding good practice. It is, nevertheless, possible to distinguish some key components of the more promising approaches.

Family

There are a number of features that promising family support projects are seen to share. These include:

- a clear grasp of who the service is designed to help and at what stage(s) of children's development

- appropriate targeting – only the most intensive services are targeted on individuals and families known to social services and/or the police. Other initiatives are targeted geographically on neighbourhoods, avoiding the counter-productive stigma of labelling individual families and children

- appropriate location – an open-access family centre is not stigmatising to families in the way that a local social services office might be. Schools may also be viewed positively as a base for parenting education and support services

- an emphasis on building parental confidence and competence from existing strengths

- encouraging parents to share their own experiences and expertise rather than depending entirely on professional instruction

- ability to co - operate and work collaboratively with other agencies.

Schools

The amount of anti - social and criminal behaviour that a school experiences will be partly determined by the family backgrounds and abilities of the pupils it admits.

Children from disadvantaged backgrounds clearly benefit from high quality pre-school programmes whose features include:

- a curriculum that encourages active learning and promotes children's sense of self - control and self - discipline;

- involvement of parents (including home visiting) to ensure that active learning is reinforced

- a staff to child ratio of no more than one to ten.

Some schools have fewer behaviour problems and lower levels of delinquency among their pupils, despite having comparable intakes (Rutter et al., 1979; Mortimore et al., 1988). Since children's low achievement and disruptive behaviour in school are two of the main factors linked to later criminality, it might be assumed that the best way for schools to improve their performance would be to identify individuals at risk for remedial attention. There is, however, a growing body of evidence which suggests that measures targeting underachieving and disaffected pupils are not enough. Schools wishing to increase their effectiveness need to adopt an holistic approach, re-examining their curriculum, teaching methods, administration, environment and overall ethos.

The ingredients of a 'whole - school' policy can be adjusted to take account of the circumstances and priorities within individual schools. Where the aim is one of improving the overall effectiveness of schools, the areas requiring scrutiny will include:

- the quality of leadership provided by head and deputy head teachers

- the involvement and commitment of all staff, including non-teaching posts

- teaching methods – including lesson structure and techniques for keeping pupil attention and maintaining order in ways that encourage learning

- curriculum content – including the use of material relevant to preventing anti-social behaviour (ranging from social skills training and remedial education to sessions concerned with relevant issues such as bullying, drug abuse, crime and citizenship)

- discipline – ensuring that school rules are fair and backed by effective sanctions that are consistently applied

- environment – minimising the extent to which playgrounds, corridors and other physical features contribute to anti-social behaviour, bullying and truancy

- administration – improved record keeping and information processing methods can ensure that problems are tackled at the earliest possible stage (for example, same-day contact with the parents of suspected truants)

- parent involvement and pupil consultation – there is evidence that a partnership between parents and schools can help raise standards of academic achievement and behaviour (Graham and Utting, 1996) Pupils can, likewise, play a positive part in reducing bullying and other anti-social behaviour provided they have the opportunity to contribute (Smith and Sharp, 1994).

Sport and Leisure

Although it has long been assumed that sports, outdoor pursuits and constructive leisure activities have a part to play in reducing criminality, it is difficult to argue that such activities have in themselves a generalisable influence on criminality. The lack of empirical research means important practice issues remain unresolved. For example:

- which interventions work best with particular age groups

- what mix of ingredients within programmes is most effective in working with:

  - young people in general

  - unconvicted youth, 'at risk' of criminal involvement

  - young people who have only recently begun to offend

  - recidivist juvenile offenders.

- whether programmes work better with a mix of offenders and non-offenders or with a segregated group

- whether there are particular sports, outdoor and leisure activities that are more effective than others when pursued as part of an overall programme.

A stronger case exists for regarding the discipline, cognitive skills and social interaction demanded by many sporting and leisure activities as useful ingredients in wider ranging prevention initiatives. The most promising programmes are currently those that are:

- concerned with other aspects of young people's everyday lives, including school attendance, training opportunities and job-search

- inclusive of follow-up work with participants in their own communities.

- not only able to furnish some evidence of positive outcomes, but also governed by a clear rationale and strategy for achieving their objectives.

There is a shortage of conclusive evidence regarding the contribution that more conventional youth work can make to crime and criminality prevention. Recent publications, including conclusions derived from evaluation of the DfEE GEST Youth Action schemes, nevertheless, suggest that the most effective programmes are those that:

- are based on a careful assessment of local needs

- lead to practical, straightforward plans whose intended outcomes are clearly and simply defined

- include an explanation of how the proposed methods will reduce the likelihood of young people committing offences

- target priority groups and individuals at risk and identify the methods by which they will be contacted

- are implemented by qualified youth workers with the skills to build relationships of trust with young people

- seek multi-agency involvement, with a clear sense of its purpose

- involve young people themselves in the planning, implementation and evaluation stages so that they can recognise and 'own' their learning from the programme (Dept. for Education and Education, 1996b; Huskins, 1996).

Cost effectiveness

There is little detailed evidence in the UK regarding the cost effectiveness of criminality reduction programmes. In the United States, it is calculated that every dollar invested in the 1960s Perry Pre-School Programme saved $7 in real terms for the taxpayer. This suggests that even a relatively expensive preventive intervention of high quality can prove remarkably cost effective in the long term. Another recent set of American calculations suggests that parenting education and incentives for low-income students to complete their (high school) education could be particularly cost-effective in reducing serious crime (Greenwood, 1996).

Although the cost figures given for projects in this report are unrefined and do not allow direct comparisons, it will be seen that the most expensive programmes are generally those designed to tackle the most extreme cases of anti-social behaviour and dysfunctional families. Yet their costs may still represent good value compared with a placement in local authority accommodation or custody. They also emphasise the advantages of trying to prevent problems before they reach crisis point by implementing less expensive interventions at an earlier stage.

Strategic interventions

This report has focused on individual descriptions of projects that are relevant to reducing criminality among young people. This does not mean that they work best when applied in isolation. On the contrary, the last and arguably most important conclusion to be drawn about best practice is that multiple problems demand multiple solutions. In other words, communities wishing to reduce the risks of their young people turning to crime are advised to adopt a strategic approach, combining 'early years' initiatives with schools effectiveness programmes and mixing family support services with constructive pursuits for young people.

The benefits of analysing crime problems in a locality and then tackling the priorities with a range of different preventive measures are recognised in the Government's *Safer Cities* initiative. Schemes are not only founded on a partnership of local interests, but also require a degree of multi-agency co-operation for their implementation. Increasingly, too, they include projects whose acknowledged aim is criminality reduction.

Such developments are assisted in the UK by progress in understanding how agencies can work constructively together. For example, the *Pen Green Centre* in Corby is an established and much-praised example of co-operation between social services and education. But progress towards proper implementation of the Children Act will increasingly demand joint working between the statutory services and partnerships with specialist voluntary organisations, like those described in this report (Audit Commission, 1994). Some local authorities have taken significant steps towards achieving a multi-disciplinary approach. Hackney, for example, has published a Children's Plan, written in plain English, which surveys the need for children's services within the borough, details current provision and sets out the authority's plans to further implement the Children Act (London Borough of Hackney,

1994). Research has also started to consider the organisational arrangements and practices that make multi-agency working more effective.[1]

One example of a criminality reduction strategy that is being widely replicated throughout the United States is the *Communities that Care* programme devised by Prof. J. David Hawkins and colleagues at the University of Washington, Seattle. It has evolved in recent years from a programme targeting young people's substance abuse to a wider focus on preventing anti-social behaviour. It now represents a major component in the Federal Government's Comprehensive Strategy for Serious, Violent and Chronic Juvenile Offenders (Office of Juvenile Justice and Delinquency Prevention, 1995). Its main features include:

- a strong conceptual framework, linking social behaviour to the bonds that children form with their parents, their schools, their friends and their communities

- insistence on securing active support from the 'key leaders' in a community who will assume ownership of the programme

- a detailed assessment of the incidence of relevant risk and protective factors in the community as well as existing resources to identify priority areas for action

- the implementation of interventions whose effectiveness has already been established by research (Developmental Research and Programs Inc., 1994).

Although it has received Federal funding for implementation in all 50 states, *Communities that Care* has yet to be rigorously evaluated as a package. Even so, its combination of a systematic approach with in-built flexibility towards local circumstances provides a useful and replicable model. (Farrington, 1996).

The experience of *Safer Cities* in Britain as well as *Communities that Care* in the United States suggests that criminality prevention strategies will work best when they are:

- targeted geographically on identifiable communities

- based on a strong commitment between social services, education, the youth service, police and other key organisations to multi-agency co-operation

---

1. For example, a study of inter-agency working with teenagers with multiple problems in Oxford, Roaf, C. & Lloyd, C. (1995) *Multi agency work with young peoiple in difficulty.* Social Care Research Findings No 68. Joseph Rowntree Foundation. Also described in Utting, D. (1995).

- guided by a detailed audit of local risk factors and of the existing resources that are relevant to reducing them.

Having identified the priority risks to be addressed within their communities, local managers should, so far as possible, base their choice of interventions on programmes with a track record of success. For any particular approach they should be able to:

- specify which risk factors and which problem behaviours they are seeking to reduce

- provide a reasoned explanation of how the chosen intervention(s) are expected to achieve the desired outcomes

There is a case for placing criminality reduction strategies on a separate footing from other crime prevention measures. This is primarily because of the very extensive range of benefits that such a programme can reasonably be expected to confer. The projects described in this report are relevant to children's health, education, employment prospects and general behaviour as well as their chances of becoming criminally involved. Taken together, they are not just about crime prevention, but a wider ability to build a more cohesive and healthier society.

Appendix 1

Project addresses/contact numbers

Chapter 2: Families

Exploring Parenthood,
The National Parenting Development Centre,
4 Ivory Place,
Treadgold Street,
London W11 4BP
Tel: 0171-221 4471

Kids Clubs Network,
Bellerive House,
3 Muirfield Crescent,
London E14 9SZ
Tel: 0171-512 2112

Parent Network,
44-46 Caversham Road,
London NW5 2DS
Tel: 0171-485 8535

Parents as Teachers
King's Wood County First School
Totteridge Lane
High Wycombe
Buckinghamshire HP13 7LR
Tel: 01494 527153

Home-Start UK,
2 Salisbury Road,
Leicester LE1 7QR
Tel: 0116-233 9955

Pen Green Centre,
Pen Green Lane,
Corby,
Northamptonshire NN17 1BJ
Tel: 01536 400068

West Leeds Family Service Unit,
3 Chiswick Street,
Leeds LS6 1QE
Tel: 0113-275 7600

Dr Stephen Scott,
Consultant in Child and Adolescent Psychiatry,
Institute of Psychiatry,
De Crespigny Park,
Denmark Hill,
London SE5 8AF
Tel: 0171-703 5411

Family Nurturing Network,
Unit 12F, Minns Estate,
7 West Way,
Botley Road,
Oxford OX2 0JD
Tel: 01865 722442

Dr Christine Puckering,
(Mellow Parenting),
Wester Craigend,
Polmaise Road
Stirling, FK7 9PX
Tel: 01786 475025

National NEWPIN,
Sutherland House,
35 Sutherland Square,
London SE17 3EE
Tel: 0171-703 6326

NCH–Action for Children,
(Radford Shared Care Project),
East Midlands Office,
28 Magdala Road,
Nottingham NG3 5DF.
Tel: 0115-962 2650

NCH–Action for Children,
(Young Offender Community Support Scheme),
South East Regional Office,
158 Crawley Road,
Roffey,
Horsham,
West Sussex RH12 4EU.
Tel: 01403 225900

Fostering and Adoption Section,
(Community Placement Scheme),
Cardiff County Council,
Trowbridge Centre,
Greenway Road,
Rhymney,
Cardiff.
Tel: 01222 774600

Margaret Carter,
(Community Placement Scheme),
Vale of Glamorgan Social Services,
91 Salisbury Road,
Barry,
Vale of Glamorgan.
Tel: 01446 745820

High/Scope UK,
Copperfield House,
190-192 Maple Road,
London SE20 8HT
Tel: 0181-676 0220

Cities in Schools (UK),
Lincoln House,
The Paddocks,
347 Cherry Hinton Road,
Cambridge CB1 4DH.
Tel: 01223 242849

Education Department,
(Dorset Health Alliance),
Dorset House,
20-22 Christchurch Road,
Dorset BH1 3NL.
Tel: 01202 221216

Education Department,
(Sheffield Anti-Bullying Initiative),
Sheffield City Council,
Leopold Street,
Sheffield S1 1RJ
Tel: 0114-272 6341

Schools Crime Awareness and Reduction Programme (SCARP)
21 Upper Beveridge Way,
Newton Aycliffe,
Co. Durham DL5 4ED.
Tel: 01325 300441

Inner London Probation Service,
(Ilderton Motor Project),
71-73 Great Peter Street,
London SW1P 2BN
Tel: 0171-222 5656

Millwall Community Sports Scheme,
The Den,
Zampa Road,
London SE16 3HL.
Tel: 0171-231 0379

S.P.A.C.E. Coordinator,
Staffordshire Police HQ,
Cannock Road,
Stafford ST17 0QG.
Tel: 01785 257717

Sheila Duggan,
(Peterborough City L.I.N.C.),
Community Education Project Co-ordinator,
Cambridgeshire County Council,
Gazeley House,
Princes Street,
Huntingdon PE18 6NS
Tel: 01480 425517

Sports Counselling Scheme,
27a Hanover Buildings,
Southampton S014 1JU.
Tel: 01703 638037

West Yorkshire Sports Counselling Association,
Calderdale Leisure in Action Unit,
Calderdale Sports Stadium,
The Shay,
Shaw Hill,
Halifax HX1 2YT.
Tel: 01422 330383

Yorkshire Adventure Sports,
17a Beech Grove,Harrogate,
North Yorkshire HG2 0EX.
Tel: 01423 522649

Fairbridge,
1 Westminster Bridge Road,
London SE1 7PL.
Tel: 0171-928 1704

Outward Bound Trust,
Watermillock,
Penrith,
Cumbria CA11 0JL
Tel: 0990 134227

Mobex,
88 Sheil Road,
Liverpool L6 3AF.
Tel: 0151-263 0557

Cheshire Youth Service,
(Runcorn Youth Action Project),
Education Services Group,
County Hall,
Chester CH1 1SF.
Tel: 01244 602350

Tony Allen,
(Welland Youth Action),
Patch Co-ordinator,,
Cambridgeshire Community Education,
Peterborough Centre for Multi-Cultural Education,
165a Cromwell Road,
Peterborough PE1 2EL
Tel: 01733 896280

Youth at Risk (UK),
Central Administration Office,
Bovingdon,
Marlow Common,
Buckinghamshire SL7 2QR.
Tel: 01628 481814

References

Audit Commission (1994). *Seen But Not Heard. Co-ordinating Community Child Health and Social Services for Children in Need.* HMSO.

Baginsky, M. (1993). *Parent Link in Waltham Forest: an evaluation.* Baginsky Associates and Waltham Forest LEA .

Barnett, W.S.(1994). *Cost-Benefit Analysis* in L.J. Schweinhart et al. (1993).

Barrett, J. (1996). *A Review of Research Literature Relating to Outdoor Adventure and Personal and Social Development with Young Offenders and Young People at Risk.* Foundation for Outdoor Adventure.

Barrett, J. (1996) See also Barrett, J. (1994) Adventure-Based Interventions With Young People in Trouble and At Risk. (Proceedings of a National One-Day Conference and a Study Weekend.) Basecamp.

Bates, G. (1993). *The effectiveness of adventurous outdoor pursuits courses as a medium for positive relationship building.* Unpublished doctoral thesis, University of Birmingham.

Bavolek, J.S. (1984). *An Innovated Program for Reducing Abusive Parent-Child Interactions.* Child Resource World Review, No2., pp. 6-24.

Berrueta-Clement, J.R., Schweinhart, L.J., Barnett, W.S., Epstein, A.S. & Weikart, D.P. (1984). *Changed Lives. The Effects of the Perry Preschool Program on Youths Through Age 19.* High/Scope Press.

Braffington, S. (1996). *Evaluation of a Nurturing Programme.* Unpublished doctoral thesis.

Burnell, A. (1995). *Developing work and family services in the workplace.* Social Policy Research Findings no 69, Joseph Rowntree Foundation.

Butler, S. (1994/5/6). *Radford Shared Care Project – Research Reports* Centre for Social Action, School of Social Studies, University of Nottingham.

Cambridgeshire County Council (1994). *The Welland Youth Action Scheme.* April 1993-March 1994 Report.

Cambridgeshire County Council (1995). Report for Peterborough City L.I.N.C. 1994.

Coalter, F. (1988). *Sport and Anti-Social Behaviour.* Research Report No.2. Scottish Sports Council.

Coopers & Lybrand (1994). *Preventative Strategy for Young People in Trouble.* Report for the ITV Telethon / Prince's Trust.

Cox, A.D., Puckering, C., Pound, A., Mills, M. & Owen A.L. (1990). *The evaluation of a home-visiting and befriending scheme: NEWPIN.* Final research report to the Department of Health.

Crime Concern (1995). *The Prevention of Criminality.* A briefing paper for crime prevention partnerships. Swindon.

Dartington Social Research Unit (1993). *Taking forward specialist services for young offenders.* The Hampshire Young Offender Community Support Scheme.

Davis, H. (1996). *An Independent Evaluation of Parent-Link.* Parent Network.

Department for Education (1994). *Bullying: don't suffer in silence.* An anti bullying pack for schools. HMSO (accompanying training video from DfE/Dialogue Productions (Wolverhampton)).

Dept. for Education and Employment (1996a). *The Out of School Initiative.* Second Evaluation undertaken by OPCS / Institute for Employment Studies.

Dept. for Education and Employment (1996b). *Grants for Education Training and Support GEST 11: Youth Service.* Circular to Chief Education Officers 19/7/96.

Dept. of Education and Science (1991). *Adventure Experiences for Young People from Urban Areas.* A report by HMI. 93/91/NS

Dept. of Education and Science/Welsh Office (1989). *Discipline in Schools.* Report of the Committee of Enquiry chaired by Lord Elton. HMSO.

Department of Health (1991) *The Children Act 1989. Guidance and Regulations Vol.2.* HMSO.

De Souza, M. (1994). *Parental Education and 'Parents Against Crime' and 'Parents First' Project* in C. Henricson (ed). Crime and the Family Conference report. London: Family Policy Studies Centre.

Developmental Research and Programs Inc. (1994). *Communities that Care: Risk-Focussed Prevention Using the Social Development Strategy.* (Seattle).

Diverse Productions (1994). *Tough Love.* Channel 4 documentary.

Exploring Parenthood (1995). *Moyenda Project Report 1991-1994.*

Fairbridge (1995). *Help Yourself Get Set for the Future.* Corporate pack.

Farrington, D.P. (1993). *Understanding and Preventing Bullying* in M. Tonry (ed) Crime and Justice Vol.17. University of Chicago Press.

Farrington, D.P. (1996). *Understanding and Preventing Youth Crime* Joseph Rowntree Foundation/York Publishing services.

Fleming, J. & Ward, D. (1992). *"For the Children to be Alright their Mothers Need to be Alright" An alternative to removing the child: The Radford Shared Care Project.* An evaluation from the participants' viewpoints. Centre for Social Action, School of Social Studies, University of Nottingham.

Forehand, R.L. & McMahon, R.J. (1981). *Helping the Noncompliant Child: a clinician's guide to parent training.* Guilford Press (New York).

Frost, N., Johnson, L., Wallis, L. & Stein, M. (1996). *Negotiated Friendship: Home-Start and Family Support.* Home-Start UK.

Fyfe, K. (1990). *Outdoor pursuits courses for young offenders and 'at risk' youth.* Unpublished report. New Zealand Department of Justice. Cited in Barrett, J. (1996).

Galloway, D. & Smith, M. (Unpublished). *Education and Prevention of Crime (EPOC) Evaluation.* Home Office.

Gent, M. (1992). *Parenting assessment: The parent/child game.* Nursing Standard Vol. 6, No 29, pp 31-35.

Gibbons, J. & Thorpe, S. (1989). *Can Voluntary Support Projects Help Vulnerable Families? The Work of Home-Start.* British Journal of Social Work 19, pp 189-202.

Graham, J. (1988). *Schools. Disruptive Behaviour and Delinquency: A Review of Research.* Home Office Research Study 96. London: HMSO.

Graham, J & Bennett, T. (1995). *Crime Prevention Strategies in Europe and North America.* European Institute for Crime Prevention and Control, (HEUNI) affiliated with the United Nations. Helsinki.

Graham, J. & Bowling, B. (1995). *Young people and crime.* Home Office Research Study 145. London: Home Office.

Graham, J. & Smith, D.I. (1994). *Diversion from Offending. The Role of the Youth Service.* Swindon: Crime Concern.

Graham, J. & Utting, D. (1996). *Families, Schools and Criminality Prevention* in T. Bennett (ed) Preventing Crime and Disorder. Targeting Strategies and Responsibilities. University of Cambridge. Institute of Criminology Cambridge Cropwood Series 1996.

Greenwood, P., Model, K.E., Rydell, C.P. & Chiesa, J. (1996). *Diverting Children from a Life of Crime. Measuring Costs and Benefits.* RAND (Santa Monica, California).

Hardiker, P., Exton, K. & Barker, M. (1991). *Policies and Practices in Preventive Child Care.* Avebury.

Haynes, W. (1993). *Measurement of Social Support.* Unpublished thesis cited in Shinman, S. (1994).

Heal, K. & Laycock G. (1987). *Preventing Juvenile Crime. The Staffordshire Experience.* Home Office

Henricson, C. (1995) *Parents Against Crime. A Pilot Project for the Parents of Juvenile Offenders. An Evaluation.* Family Policy Studies Centre.

High/ScopeUK (1995). *The First Five Years of High/Scope UK.* Pirani, M. (1994) High/Scope Pre-School Curriculum in C. Henricson (ed). Crime and the Family Conference Report. London: Family Policy Studies Centre.

Home Affairs Committee (1993). *Juvenile Offenders. Sixth report.* House of Commons.

Home Office (1995a) Probation Circular PC52/1995.

Home Office (1995b). Probation Circular PC63/1995.

Home Office Research and Statistics Department (1991). *National Prison Survey.* Research Study No. 128. London: HMSO.

Hooper, D. (1992). *MOBEX Merseyside. The Way We Work*. The Journal of Adventure Education and Outdoor Leadership 9 (3) pp. 6-8.

Howell, J.C., Krisberg, B., Hawkins, J.D., & Wilson, J.J. (1995). *A sourcebook. Serious Violent & Chronic Juvenile Offenders*. Sage.

Hunt, J. (1989). *In Search of Adventure. A Study of Opportunities for Adventure and Challenge for Young People*. Talbot Adair Press.

Huskins, J. (1995). *Youth at Risk. An objective assessment*. Briefing paper available from Youth at Risk.

Huskins, J. (1996). *Quality Work with Young People. Developing social skills and diversion from risk*. Youth Clubs UK.

Johnson, L (1993). *Families in Partnership. An Independent Evaluation of the West Leeds Family Service Unit Neighbourhood Project*. Child Care Research and Development Unit of the Department of Adult Continuing Education, University of Leeds/Family Service Units.

Jones, V. (1995). *Match of the Day. A step by step guide to setting up football projects for young people at risk*. London: The Divert Trust.

Kids' Clubs Network (1995). *The Next Step for School Age Childcare. A costed development strategy for the year 2000 and beyond*.

Kolvin, I., Miller, F.J.W., Scott, D.McI., Gatzanis, S.R.M. & Fleeting, M. (1990). *Continuities of Deprivation?* ESRC/DHSS Studies in Deprivation and Disadvantage No15. Avebury.

Lazar, I. & Darlington (1982). *The Lasting Effects of Early Education*. A Report from the Consortium of Longitudinal Studies. Monograph of the Society for Research in Child Development 47.

Learmonth, J. (1995). *More Willingly to School? An independent evaluation of the Truancy and Disaffected Pupils GEST Programme*. Department for Education and Employment.

Loeber ,R. & Dishion, T. (1983). *Early Predictors of Male Deliquency: a review*. Psychological Bulletin 94, No1, pp. 68-99.

Loeber, R. & Stouthamer-Loeber, M. (1986). *Family Factors as Correlates and Predictors of Juvenile Conduct Problems and Delinquency* in M. Tonry & N. Morris (eds) *Crime and Justice – an annual review of research*. Vol 7. University of Chicago.

London Borough of Hackney (1994). *The First Hackney Children's Plan*

Martin, J.H. & Webster, D. (1994). *Probation Motor Projects in England and Wales.* London: Home Office.

Maughan, B. (1994). *School Influences* in M.Rutter & D.F. Hay (eds) Development Through Life. A Handbook for Clinicians. Blackwell Scientific Publications.

Mills, M. & Puckering, C. (1996). *Growing pains - every parent needs some support* in D. Utting (ed.) Families and Parenting., Report of a conference held at the Royal College of Physicians, London 26th September 1995. London: Family Policy Studies Centre.

MVA Consultancy (1991). *Links between Truancy and Delinquency.* Report prepared for the Scottish Office.

Nichols, G. & Taylor, P. (1994). *West Yorkshire Sports Counselling Project.* Evaluation First Report October 1994. Calderdale: West Yorkshire Sports Counselling Association.

Nichols, G. & Taylor, P. (1996). *West Yorkshire Sports Counselling.* Final Evaluation Report. Calderdale: West Yorkshire Sports Counselling Association.

Oakley, A., Mauthner, M., Rajan, L., Stone, S. & Turner, H. (1994). *An Evaluation of NEWPIN.* Social Science Research Unit, Institute of Education, University of London.

Office for Standards in Education (1993). *Youth Work Responses to Young People at Risk.* 395/93/NS.

Office for Standards in Education (1995) *A survey of youth action schemes.* HMSO.

Office of Juvenile Justice and Delinquency Prevention (1995). *Guide for Implementing the Comprehensive Strategy for Serious, Violent and Chronic Juvenile Offenders.* (Washington D.C.).

Olweus, D. (1991). *Bully/Victim Problems Among Schoolchildren: basic facts and effects of a school-based intervention programme* in D.J. Pepler and K. Rubin (eds) The Development and Treatment of Childhood Aggression. Erlbaum (Hillsdale, New Jersey).

Osborn, A.F. (1990). *Resilient Children: a longitudinal study of high-achieving socially disadvantaged children.* Early Child Development and Care 62, pp. 23-47.

Osborn, A.F. & Millbank, J.E. (1987). *The Effects of Early Education.* Clarendon (Oxford).

Osborn, S. & West, D.J. (1978). *Effectiveness of Various Predictors of Criminal Careers.* Journal of Adolescence,1, pp. 101-117.

Outward Bound Access Programmes. 18 - month Progress Reports to the Department for Education and Employment.

Patterson, G.R. (1994a). *Some Characteristics of a Developmental Theory for Early Onset Deliquency* in J.J. Huagaard & M.F. Lenzenweger (eds) Frontiers of Developmental Psychopathology. Oxford University Press.

Patterson, G.R. (1994b). *Some Alternatives to Seven Myths about Treating Families of Antisocial Children* in C. Henricson (ed) Crime and the Family Conference Report. Proceedings of an international conference held in London 3 February 1994. London: Family Policy Studies Centre.

Pfannenstiel, J., Lambson, T. & Yarnell, V. (1991). *Second Wave Study of the Parents as Teachers Program.* Parents as Teachers National Center Inc. (St Louis, Missouri).

Pilling, D. (1990). *Escape from Disadvantage.* Falmer Press.

Pitts, J. & Smith, P. (1995). *Preventing School Bullying.* Crime Prevention and Detection Series No 63, Police Research Group. London: Home Office.

Pound, A. (1994). *NEWPIN: A Befriending and Therapeutic Network for Carers of Young Children.* HMSO / National NEWPIN.

Puckering, C., Rogers, J., Mills, M., Cox, A.D. & Mattson-Graff, M. (1994). *Mellow Mothering: Process and Evaluation of Group Intervention for Distressed Families.* Child Abuse Review, 3, pp 299-

Pugh, G., De'Ath, E. & Smith, C. (1994). *Confident Parents, Confident Children. Policy and practice in parent education and support.* National Children's Bureau.

Quickenden, K. (1996). *Family Nurturing Network in Families and Parenting.* In: D. Utting (ed.). Report of a conference held on September 26th 1995. . London: Family Policy Studies Centre/Department of Health.

Robins, D. (1990). *Sport as Prevention. The role of Sport in Crime Prevention Programmes Aimed at Young People.* Centre for Criminological Research, University of Oxford.

Robins, L. (1978). *Sturdy childhood predictors of adult anti-social behaviour: Replications from longitudinal studies.* Psychological Medicine 8, pp. 611-622.

Rutter, M. & Giller, H. (1983). *Juvenile Delinquency. Trends and Perspectives.* Penguin.

Sampson, R.J. & Laub, J.H. (1993). *Crime in the Making: Pathways and turning points through life.* Harvard University Press. (Cambridge, Mass.).

Schweinhart, L.J., Barnes, H.V & Weikart, D.P. (1993). *The High/Scope Perry Preschool Study Through Age 27.* High/Scope Educational Foundation (Ypsilanti, Michigan).

Schweinhart, L.J., Weikart, D.P. & Larner, M.B. (1986). *Consequences of Three Pre-School Curriculum Models Through Age 15.* Early Education Research Quarterly, 1 pp. 15-45.

Schweinhart, L.J. & Weikart, D.P. (forthcoming). *The High/Scope Pre-School Curriculum Comparison StudyThrough Age 23* (Preliminary findings). Ypsilanti, Michigan.

Sharp, S. & Smith, P.K. (1994). *Tackling Bullying in Your School.* A Practical Handbook. Routledge.

Shinman, S.M. (1994). Family *Album. Snapshots of Home-Start in words and pictures.* Home-Start UK (Leicester).

Smith, C. with Pugh, G. (1995). *Learning to be a Parent. A survey of group-based parenting programmes.* Family Policy Studies Centre/Joseph Rowntree Foundation.

Smith, D.J. (1995). *Youth Crime and Conduct Disorders: Trends, Patterns and Causal Explanations* in M. Rutter & D.J. Smith (eds.). Psychosocial Disorders in Young People. Time Trends and Their Causes. John Wiley & Sons.

Smith, P.K. & Sharp, S. (1994). *School Bullying. Insights and Perspectives.* Routledge.

South Glamorgan Social Services Department (1993). *Youth Justice and Adolescent Services Resources.*

South Glamorgan Social Services Department (1995). *Community Placement Scheme Annual Report 1994.*

Sports Council Research Unit (North West) (1989). *Participation Demonstration Projects.* Solent Sports Counselling Project, Hampshire Probation Service. Special Report on the Evaluation of the Project's Work April 1987-March 1989.

Staffordshire Police (1994). *A Review of S.P.A.C.E.*

Sylva, K. (1994). *The Impact of Early Learning on Children's Later Development* in Sir C. Ball. Start right: The Importance of Early Learning. London: Royal Society for the encouragement of Arts, Manufactures and Commerce (RSA).

Utting, D. (1995). Family and Parenthood. Supporting Families, Preventing Breakdown. York: Joseph Rowntree Foundation.

Utting, D., Bright, J. & Henricson, C. (1993). *Crime and the Family: Improving child-rearing and preventing delinquency.* London: Family Policy Studies Centre.

Van der Eyken, W. (1982). *Home-Start: a four year evaluation.* Home-Start UK, Leicester (revised version published 1990).

Wadsworth, M. (1979). *The Roots of Delinquency.* Martin Robertson.

Warren, C. & Hartless, J. (1996). *The Development of Out of School Care.* Family Support Network Newsletter. School of Social Work. University of East Anglia.

Webb, J. (1994). Swindon: *Runcorn Youth Action Project.* Crime Concern.

Webster-Stratton, C. (1984). *Randomized Trial of Two Parent-Training Programs for Families With Conduct-Disordered Children.* Journal of Consulting and Clinical Psychology Vol. 52, No. 4 pp. 666-678.

West, D.J. (1982). *Deliquency: its roots, careers and prospects.* Heinemann.

Whalley, M. (1994). *Learning to be Strong. Setting up a neighbourhood service for under-fives and their families.* Hodder and Stoughton.

Whild, P. (1991). *The parent/child game: A pilot study of treatment outcome and consumer satisfaction.* Unpublished cited in Gent, M. (1992).

Whitfield, D. (1995). *Partners in Crime:* article in the Fairbridge magazine Challenger.

Whitney, I., Rivers,I., Smith, P.K. & Sharp, S. (1994). *The Sheffield Project: methodology and findings* in P.K. Smith & S. Sharp (1994).

Wilkinson, J. & Morgan, D. (1995). *The Impact of Ilderton Motor Project on Motor Vehicle Crime and Offending.* Inner London Probation Service.

Winterdyk, J. & Griffiths, C. (1984). *Wilderness experience programs: reforming delinquents or beating around the bush?* Juvenile and Family Court Journal, 35 (3) pp.35-44.

Woodhead, M. (1985). *Pre-school education has long-term effects: but can they be generalised?* Oxford Review of Education. vol. 11, No 2 pp 113-155.

Youth at Risk UK (1994) Training Manual. (Marlow Common, Bucks.).

Youth at Risk UK (1995). Youth at Risk. A Community Programme. (Marlow, Bucks.).

Publications

List of research publications

A list of research reports for the last three years is provided below. A **full** list of publications is available on request from the Research and Statistics Directorate Information and Publications Group.

Home Office Research Studies (HORS)

133. **Intensive Probation in England and Wales: an evaluation.** George Mair, Charles Lloyd, Claire Nee and Rae Sibbett. 1994. xiv + 143pp. (0 11 341114 6).

134. **Contacts between Police and Public: findings from the 1992 British Crime Survey.** Wesley G Skogan. 1995. ix + 93pp. (0 11 341115 4).

135. **Policing low-level disorder: Police use of Section 5 of the Public Order Act 1986.** David Brown and Tom Ellis. 1994. ix + 69pp. (0 11 341116 2).

136. **Explaining reconviction rates: A critical analysis.** Charles Lloyd, George Mair and Mike Hough. 1995. xiv + 103pp. (0 11 341117 0).

137. **Case Screening by the Crown Prosecution Service: How and why cases are terminated.** Debbie Crisp and David Moxon. 1995. viii + 66pp. (0 11 341137 5).

138. **Public Interest Case Assessment Schemes.** Debbie Crisp, Claire Whittaker and Jessica Harris. 1995. x + 58pp. (0 11 341139 1).

139. **Policing domestic violence in the 1990s.** Sharon Grace. 1995. x + 74pp. (0 11 341140 5).

140. **Young people, victimisation and the police: British Crime Survey findings on experiences and attitudes of 12 to 15 year olds.** Natalie Aye Maung. 1995. xii + 140pp. (0 11 341150 2).

141. **The Settlement of refugees in Britain.** Jenny Carey-Wood, Karen Duke, Valerie Karn and Tony Marshall. 1995. xii + 133pp. (0 11 341145 6).

142. **Vietnamese Refugees since 1982.** Karen Duke and Tony Marshall. 1995. x + 62pp. (0 11 341147 2).

143. **The Parish Special Constables Scheme.** Peter Southgate, Tom Bucke and Carole Byron. 1995. x + 59pp. (1 85893 458 3).

144. **Measuring the Satisfaction of the Courts with the Probation Service.** Chris May. 1995. x + 76pp. (1 85893 483 4).

145. **Young people and crime.** John Graham and Benjamin Bowling. 1995. xv + 142pp. (1 85893 551 2).

146. **Crime against retail and manufacturing premises: findings from the 1994 Commercial Victimisation Survey.** Catriona Mirrlees-Black and Alec Ross. 1995. xi + 110pp. (1 85893 554 7).

147. **Anxiety about crime: findings from the 1994 British Crime Survey.** Michael Hough. 1995. viii + 92pp. (1 85893 553 9).

148. **The ILPS Methadone Prescribing Project.** Rae Sibbitt. 1996. viii + 69pp. (1 85893 485 0).

149. **To scare straight or educate? The British experience of day visits to prison for young people.** Charles Lloyd. 1996. xi + 60pp. (1 85893 570 9).

150. **Predicting reoffending for Discretionary Conditional Release.** John B Copas, Peter Marshall and Roger Tarling. 1996. vii + 49pp. (1 85893 576 8).

151. **Drug misuse declared: results of the 1994 British Crime Survey.** Malcom Ramsay and Andrew Percy. 1996. xv + 131pp. (1 85893 628 4).

152. **An Evaluation of the Introduction and Operation of the Youth Court.** David O'Mahony and Kevin Haines. 1996. viii + 70pp. (1 85893 579 2).

153. **Fitting supervision to offenders: assessment and allocation decisions in the Probation Service.** Ros Burnett. 1996. xi + 99pp. (1 85893 599 7).

154. **Ethnic minorities: victimisation and racial harassment. Findings from the 1988 and 1992 British Crime Surveys.** Marian Fitzgerald and Chris Hale. 1996. xi + 97pp. (1 85893 603 9).

156. **Automatic Conditional Release: the first two years.** Mike Maguire, Brigitte Perroud and Peter Raynor. 1996. x + 114pp. (1 85893 659 4).

157. **Testing obscenity: an international comparison of laws and controls relating to obscene material.** Sharon Grace. 1996. ix + 46pp. (1 85893 672 1).

160. Implementing crime prevention schemes in a multi-agency setting: aspects of process in the Safer Cities programme. Mike Sutton. 1996. x + 53. (1 85893 691 8).

Nos 155, 158 and 159 not published yet.

Research and Planning Unit Papers (RPUP)

81. **The welfare needs of unconvicted prisoners.** Diane Caddle and Sheila White. 1994.

82. **Racially motivated crime: a British Crime Survey analysis.** Natalie Aye Maung and Catriona Mirrlees-Black. 1994.

83. **Mathematical models for forecasting Passport demand.** Andy Jones and John MacLeod. 1994.

84. **The theft of firearms.** John Corkery. 1994.

85. **Equal opportunities and the Fire Service.** Tom Bucke. 1994.

86. **Drug Education Amongst Teenagers: a 1992 British Crime Survey Analysis.** Lizanne Dowds and Judith Redfern. 1995.

87. **Group 4 Prisoner Escort Service: a survey of customer satisfaction.** Claire Nee. 1994.

88. **Special Considerations: Issues for the Management and Organisation of the Volunteer Police.** Catriona Mirrlees-Black and Carole Byron. 1995.

89. **Self-reported drug misuse in England and Wales: findings from the 1992 British Crime Survey.** Joy Mott and Catriona Mirrlees-Black. 1995.

90. **Improving bail decisions: the bail process project, phase 1.**
John Burrows, Paul Henderson and Patricia Morgan. 1995.

91. **Practitioners' views of the Criminal Justice Act: a survey of criminal justice agencies.** George Mair and Chris May. 1995.

92. **Obscene, threatening and other troublesome telephone calls to women in England and Wales: 1982-1992.** Wendy Buck, Michael Chatterton and Ken Pease. 1995.

93. **A survey of the prisoner escort and custody service provided by Group 4 and by Securicor Custodial Services.** Diane Caddle. 1995.

Research Findings

8. **Findings from the International Crime Survey.** Pat Mayhew. 1994.

9 **Fear of Crime: Findings from the 1992 British Crime Survey.** Catriona Mirrlees-Black and Natalie Aye Maung. 1994.

10. **Does the Criminal Justice system treat men and women differently?** Carol Hedderman and Mike Hough. 1994.

11. **Participation in Neighbourhood Watch: Findings from the 1992 British Crime Survey.** Lizanne Dowds and Pat Mayhew. 1994.

12. **Explaining Reconviction Rates: A Critical Analysis.** Charles Lloyd, George Mair and Mike Hough. 1995.

13. **Equal opportunities and the Fire Service.** Tom Bucke. 1994.

14. **Trends in Crime: Findings from the 1994 British Crime Survey.** Pat Mayhew, Catriona Mirrlees-Black and Natalie Aye Maung. 1994.

15. **Intensive Probation in England and Wales: an evaluation.** George Mair, Charles Lloyd, Claire Nee and Rae Sibbitt. 1995.

16. **The settlement of refugees in Britain.** Jenny Carey-Wood, Karen Duke, Valerie Karn and Tony Marshall. 1995.

17. **Young people, victimisation and the police: British Crime Survey findings on experiences and attitudes of 12- to 15- year-olds.** Natalie Aye Maung.

18. **Vietnamese Refugees since 1982.** Karen Duke and Tony Marshall. 1995.

19. **Supervision of Restricted Patients in the Community.** Suzanne Dell and Adrian Grounds. 1995.

20. **Videotaping children's evidence: an evaluation.** Graham Davies, Clare Wilson, Rebecca Mitchell and John Milsom. 1995.

21. **The mentally disordered and the police.** Graham Robertson, Richard Pearson and Robert Gibb. 1995.

22. **Preparing records of taped interviews.** Andrew Hooke and Jim Knox. 1995.

23. **Obscene, threatening and other troublesome telephone calls to women: Findings from the British Crime Survey.** Wendy Buck, Michael Chatterton and Ken Pease. 1995.

24. **Young people and crime.** John Graham and Ben Bowling. 1995.

25. **Anxiety about crime: Findings from the 1994 British Crime Survey.** Michael Hough. 1995.

26. **Crime against retail premises in 1993.** Catriona Mirrlees-Black and Alec Ross. 1995.

27. **Crime against manufacturing premises in 1993.** Catriona Mirrlees-Black and Alec Ross. 1995.

28. **Policing and the public: findings from the 1994 British Crime Survey.** Tom Bucke. 1995.

29. **The Child Witness Pack – An Evaluation.** Joyce Plotnikoff and Richard Woolfson. 1995.

30. **To scare straight or educate? The British experience of day visits to prison for young people.** Charles Lloyd. 1996.

31. **The ADT drug treatment programme at HMP Downview – a preliminary evaluation.** Elaine Player and Carol Martin. 1996.

32. **Wolds remand prison – an evaluation.** Keith Bottomley, Adrian James, Emma Clare and Alison Liebling. 1996.

33. **Drug misuse declared: results of the 1994 British Crime Survey.** Malcolm Ramsay and Andrew Percy. 1996.

34. **Crack cocaine and drugs-crime careers.** Howard Parker and Tim Bottomley. 1996.

35. **Imprisonment for fine default.** David Moxon and Claire Whittaker. 1996.

36. **Fine impositions and enforcement following the Criminal Justice Act 1993.** Elizabeth Charman, Bryan Gibson, Terry Honess and Rod Morgan. 1996.

37. **Victimisation in prisons.** Ian O'Donnell and Kimmett Edgar. 1996.

39. **Ethnic minorities, victimisation and racial harassment.** Marian Fitzgerald and Chris Hale. 1996.

40. **Evaluating joint performance management between the police and the Crown Prosecution Service.** Andrew Hooke, Jim Knox and David Portas. 1996.

43. **Pakistani women's experience of domestic violence in Great Britain.** Salma Choudry. 1996.

45. **Does treating sex offenders reduce reoffending?** Carol Hedderman and Darren Sugg. 1996.

Research Bulletin

The Research Bulletin is published twice each year and contains short articles on recent research.

Occasional Papers

Measurement of caseload weightings associated with the Children Act. Richard J. Gadsden and Graham J. Worsdale. 1994. (Available from the RSD Information and Publications Group).

Managing difficult prisoners: The Lincoln and Hull special units. Professor Keith Bottomley, Professor Norman Jepson, Mr Kenneth Elliott and Dr Jeremy Coid. 1994. (Available from the RSD Information and Publications Group).

The Nacro diversion initiative for mentally disturbed offenders: an account and an evaluation. Home Office, NACRO and Mental Health Foundation. 1994. (Available from the RSD Information and Publications Group).

Probation Motor Projects in England and Wales. J P Martin and Douglas Martin. 1994.

Community-based treatment of sex offenders: an evaluation of seven treatment programmes. R Beckett, A Beech, D Fisher and A S Fordham. 1994.

Videotaping children's evidence: an evaluation. Graham Davies, Clare Wilson, Rebecca Mitchell and John Milsom. 1995.

Managing the needs of female prisoners. Allison Morris, Chris Wilkinson, Andrea Tisi, Jane Woodrow and Ann Rockley. 1995.

Local information points for volunteers. Michael Locke, Nick Richards, Lorraine Down, Jon Griffiths and Roger Worgan. 1995.

Mental disorder in remand prisoners. Anthony Maden, Caecilia J. A. Taylor, Deborah Brooke and John Gunn. 1996.

An evaluation of prison work and training. Frances Simon and Claire Corbett. 1996.

The Impact of the National Lottery on the Horse-Race Betting Levy. Simon Field. 1996.

Books

Analysing Offending. Data, Models and Interpretations. Roger Tarling. 1993. viii + 203pp. (0 11 341080 8).

The Nacro diversion initiative for mentally disturbed offenders: an account and an evaluation. Home Office, NACRO and Mental Health Foundation. 1994. (Available from the RSD Information and Publications Group).

Probation Motor Projects in England and Wales. J P Martin and Douglas Martin. 1994.

Community-based treatment of sex offenders: an evaluation of seven treatment programmes. R Beckett, A Beech, D Fisher and A S Fordham. 1994.

Videotaping children's evidence: an evaluation. Graham Davies, Clare Wilson, Rebecca Mitchell and John Milsom. 1995.

Managing the needs of female prisoners. Allison Morris, Chris Wilkinson, Andrea Tisi, Jane Woodrow and Ann Rockley. 1995.

Local information points for volunteers. Michael Locke, Nick Richards, Lorraine Down, Jon Griffiths and Roger Worgan. 1995.

Mental disorder in remand prisoners. Anthony Maden, Caecilia J. A. Taylor, Deborah Brooke and John Gunn. 1996.

An evaluation of prison work and training. Frances Simon and Claire Corbett. 1996.

The Impact of the National Lottery on the Horse-Race Betting Levy. Simon Field. 1996.

Books

Analysing Offending. Data, Models and Interpretations. Roger Tarling. 1993. viii + 203pp. (0 11 341080 8).

Requests for Publications

Home Office Research Studies from 143 onwards, *Research and Planning Unit Papers, Research Findings and Research Bulletins* are available **subject to availability** on request from:

Research and Statistics Directorate
Information and Publications Group
Room 1308, Home Office
Apollo House
36 Wellesley Road
Croydon CR9 3RR
Telephone: 0181 760 8340
Fascimile: 0181 760 8364
Internet: http/www.open.gov.u/home_off/rsdhome.htm
E-mail: rsd.ha apollo @ gtnet.gov.u.

Occasional Papers can be purchased from:
Home Office
Publications Unit
50 Queen Anne's Gate
London SW1H 9AT
Telephone: 0171 273 2302

Home Office Research Studies prior to 143 can be purchased from:

HMSO Publications Centre

(Mail, fax and telephone orders only)
PO Box 276, London SW8 5DT
Telephone orders: 0171-873 9090
General enquiries: 0171-873 0011
(queuing system in operation for both numbers)
Fax orders: 0171-873 8200

*And also from **HMSO Bookshops***